Ghosts, Spirits & the Afterlife in Native American Folklore and Religion

Case Studies in Religion:
Native American Traditions – Ghosts & Spirits

Gary R. Varner

ISBN: 978-0-557-48010-4

Visit the author's website:
www.authorsden.com/garyrvarner

An OakChylde Book
Published in the United States by Lulu Press, Inc.
Raleigh, NC

Title page photograph by Gary R. Varner: Hopi petroglyph of concentric
circles representing the whirlwind and the supernatural power of ghosts.
Cover photograph by Gary R. Varner: Owens Valley Paiute rock art
depiction of an eagle shield.

Contents

Index   117

Owens Valley Paiute Rock Art of a "killed" man.

Preface

Death. We deny it. We fear it. Some of us welcome it. No matter what age we live in we keep the traditional feelings for our departed. We try to ease the soul into the afterworld as best we can. "Celebrations of life" provide a time for friends and loved ones to gather, share food and stories and grieve. Some who pass on are cremated to free the soul. Some are buried believing that the body will not become corrupted but will survive until the final judgment day. "Grave goods" are still commonly buried or are cremated as well with the body.

In contemporary Chinese society paper reproductions of cell phones, iPads, pc's, homes, cars and other things we value in life are purchased by mourners to burn and to send "up" so that the dead will not be deprived in the afterworld.

While we believe we are more advanced than those who lived before us, be they Native Americans or not, we actually do the same things they did to honor and to provide for our deceased loved ones. We are not so very different after all.

This book provides a brief survey of how America's first people reacted to death, how they disposed of their dead, their thoughts about the spirit world and the possibilities of being reborn. I believe we will see ourselves in these pages as well. Death is a part of the life process and cannot be ignored. We can, however, come to terms with it and prepare ourselves to accept it with grace and wonder. It is, after all, simply the beginning of another existence, new experiences and growth.

The belief in ghosts and spirits is universal, as is the fear that they generate. Each culture, each society has its own special perception concerning ghosts and spirits. Such a perception may include ways to appease them, ways to avoid them, and even ways to use them.

Ghosts manifest themselves in dreams, as amorphous objects, as "full body apparitions" and as animals. They can give advice, provide comfort and cause all sorts of mischief and harm. And, strangely enough, their characteristics are nearly identical from one culture to another. Native American concepts of the afterlife are also not so different from other cultural traditions, although the afterworld may be the Milky Way or underground!

This book is the second in a series of monographs focusing on specific subjects concerning cultural traditions. The first in the series is *Magic, Witchcraft, Pagans & Christians: A Study in the Suppression of Belief and the Rise of Christianity.* Future monographs will be concerned with sacred water, amulets and charms, symbols and the development of religions.

1 What Are Ghost? A Cross-Cultural Survey

Ghosts![1] The word alone creates images of translucent and flowing spirits, spirits that have either failed to realize that they are no longer physically alive, who wish to visit their friends and family or who intend to exact revenge from those left living. Ghosts are feared the world over, and have been since humans began to recognize realities and dimensions outside of the present one. Are they creations of our own minds?

Ghosts come in all shapes, sizes and forms. All of these characteristics are fluid and interchangeable at will. As previously discussed, the white owl is perhaps the most universal representation of ghosts among Native American groups. The owl is believed to be the materialization of the ghost of a malicious human being and indicates an evil intent when seen or heard. "Ghost sickness," also called "owl sickness" occurs when its call is heard. It is believed by the Apache that the owl's call will enter the body and cause sickness.

"And so to prevent sickness," Opler noted, "if an owl cried around the camp, they set fire to a stick of wood, carried it outside, and threw it in the direction of the owl. Then it stopped [hooting]." [2]

Ghostly apparitions may be caused by a phenomenon noted by the Chumash of "seeing people who aren't there." According to Chumash belief, when a person is near death, or simply sleeping, the spirit may leave the body and be seen in another location. These out-of-body events must be taken as warnings however for death will soon occur unless preventative measures are taken. Such measures may take the form of a certain ritual dance.

---

[1] The word "ghost" is a derivative of the Middle English "goste" and the German "geist," both meaning "breath". The breath leaving the body at the time of death was believed to be the soul.

[2] Opler, Morris Edward. *An Apache Life-Way: The Economic, Social, and Religious Institutions of the Chiricahua Indians.* Chicago: The University of Chicago Press 1941, 42.

Native American lore is filled with legends about ghosts and the Otherworld that they inhabit. Traditionally Native Americans have been intimately linked with nature and the world of spirit — including those beings that reside in the spirit world. To the Plains Indian, however, the interaction between humans, ghosts and spirits is considered "a normal part of life on this earth." [3] Sickness is not the result of a virus or bacteria but more likely than not, the result of "ghost illnesses" caused intentionally by a malignant spirit of a departed individual. Ghosts most often appear in dreams rather than in the physical world, although physical manifestations such as footprints and sounds are also part of their calling cards. Ideally, if such spirits want to continue their existence they should stay in the "underworld" and live a parallel existence, unaware of and inaccessible to those still living in the physical world. But folklore has many models for exceptions to this plan. The owl was considered one of the manifestations of an evil spirit, a vengeful spirit. To see an owl at night meant that a spirit had announced an evil intent. To the Chiricahua Apache, "the bad ones go right into the owl, at death, at once. The others who were good through life go to the underworld." [4]

The image of the ghost appearing as a white amorphous shape is common the world over — including among Native Americans. Opler related one such sighting by an Apache man:

"One day, after I was married, I was riding my mule back from Whitetail....We got lost in the woods and could not get out before dark. We got into a canyon neither of us knew. And up among the trees I saw something white. I didn't think anything of it, but in a few minutes I saw it again." [5]

This sighting affected the man so much that he was incapacitated for some time after he was able to return to his home.

Ghosts appear in dreams usually with the same intent — to draw the person into death. There was a belief even during the early part of the twentieth century that to see the ghost of an Indian

---

[3] St. Pierre, Mark and Tilda Long Soldier. *Walking in the Sacred Manner.* New York: Touchstone Books 1995, 108.

[4] Opler, Morris Edward. *An Apache Life-Way: The Economic, Social, and Religious Institutions of the Chiricahua Indians.* Chicago: The University of Chicago Press 1941, 230

[5] Ibid., 232.

was fatal but to see the ghost of a white man would only bring sickness.

The Lakota Sioux believed that to see a ghost would not result in harm, but "if they hear a ghost, bad luck will follow. If they hear a ghost mourning, then someone of the family will die soon."[6] To the Lakota the ghost may signify a future event, either success of a war party, or its failure. According to Walker, "if they sing the song of victory the party will succeed, but if they mourn, then the party had better go home." [7]

Ghosts were believed to inhabit abandoned camps and tipis, and sacrifices were often made to them before a war party set out to ensure the aid of the ghosts.

Ghosts are primarily interested in securing the deaths of people they knew in life; however, they also did other types of mischief, such as causing children to spill hot soup or coffee at meals.

To the Lakota the spirit is not what constitutes life; rather it is the ghost that defines life. "His ghost is his breath," they say. [8] The good spirit goes to the spirit world which is "at the other end of the spirit way," where it is never cold and hunger no longer exists and work is no longer necessary. The bad spirit does not go on to this land but stays behind in its ghost form.

Among the Oglala Sioux, ghosts are understood to attempt to entice the living to join them — only because they grieve for them and want to be with them once again. This is especially true in the period immediately after death. According to anthropologist William Powers, the loved ones of the deceased will attempt to appease the ghost by "keeping" it for one year. This is done by "feeding" [9] the ghost spirit. After a year the ghost is fed for the last time and it departs along the "ghost road," which is the Milky Way. It is said, "the aura of the Milky Way is caused by their campfires." [10]

The purpose of this ghost keeping is, according to Powers, "so that by the proper rites it will be assured a return to its origin, and

---

[6] Walker, James R. *Lakota Belief and Ritual.* Lincoln: University of Nebraska Press 1991, 104

[7] Ibid.

[8] Ibid.

[9] "Feeding" was done by placing food in a hole in the ground near the body.

[10] Powers, William K. *Oglala Religion.* Lincoln: University of Nebraska Press 1982, 53.

because the lingering ghost will help people to be mindful of death."[11]

After the Wounded Knee massacre at Pine Ridge in 1890 the United States called for "all Oglalas who were currently ghost keeping to release their souls on an appointed day."[12]

The contrast between the Apache, the Lakota Sioux and the Oglala Sioux is striking. The Apache fear the ghosts, which they believe to cause death, while the Sioux "keep" them for a time to stay near their loved ones, who will help the spirit find its way along the ghost road to the spirit world.

Ghosts were also greatly feared by the Navajo. "Ghosts are," wrote anthropologist Clyde Kluckhohn, "the witches of the world of the dead, a shadowy impalpable world altogether beyond the control of the living." [13] "Fear of ghosts," wrote anthropologist Harold E. Driver, "is intense; no matter how affectionate, helpful, and friendly a person has been while alive, his ghost is always potentially dangerous. Any slip in the complicated burial routine will offend the ghost and cause it to hover around the grave, or the house where it lived while alive, in order to take revenge on the wrongdoer." [14]

Only those who die of old age, the stillborn, or infants who die before they are able to utter a sound do not become ghosts in Navajo belief. Ghosts are, according to the Navajo, the "malignant" parts of the human spirit. To the Navajo Ghosts are capable of entering the body through the body's layers, or "interstices"—the whorls of the fingertips and hair spirals or through the mouth, nose, or ears. Ghosts are to be feared according to the Navajo. "Ghosts are inexorable," wrote anthropologist Gladys Reichard, "they cannot be persuaded to become helpful to man...the best man can do is to drive them off or avoid them." [15]

---

[11] Ibid., 93.

[12] Ibid., 122.

[13] Kluckhohn, Clyde and Dorothea Leighton. *The Navaho.* Garden City: Anchor Books/The American Museum of Natural History 1962, 184.

[14] Driver, Harold E. *Indians of North America, 2nd edition.* Chicago: University of Chicago Press 1969, 409.

[15] Reichard, Gladys A. *Navaho Religion: A Study of Symbolism.* Princeton: Princeton University Press 1950, 49.

While they may shape-shift into animal forms, such as coyotes, owls, fire, mice or even whirlwinds, they normally appear as black or very dark shapes. "Whistling in the dark," wrote Clyde Kluckhohn, "is always evidence that a ghost is near."[16] (It occurs to me that whistling, a fairly penetrating sound, is quite a natural way for humans to announce their presence — which is generally a far safer practice than surprising a wild animal in the dark! It certainly seems to be a common reaction in response to the instinctive fear that sometimes attends a walk in the dark.)

To the Cheyenne, ghosts originate with the dead but they are not spirits of particular individuals. According to anthropologist E. Adamson Hoebel, they are more poltergeists than spirit. "They make their presence known by whistling and making weird noises; in very dark places, especially in the woods, they tug at one's robe; they tap and scratch on lodge coverings. In other words, they are the night noises and sensations that make even the most skeptical of us a bit jumpy..." [17]

However, the Cheyenne do believe in individual spirits. Or rather, they believe in individual souls. Everyone dwells in a heaven after the spirit separates from the body according to Cheyenne belief. The soul, the *tasoom*, is the very nature, the very essence of the body and death is simply the next existence.

Illnesses have long been thought to be caused by vengeful ghosts. In ancient Mesopotamia, according to Thomsen, "The reason for a ghost to appear was mostly assumed to be irregularities during funerary rites or the cessation of the offerings to the dead....The ghost of someone who had died in an accident, of a criminal who might have been sentenced to death or of someone who had not been buried at all was especially likely to persecute the living." [18]

A cause and effect relationship between dissatisfied ghosts and the illness and death of an individual was a universal concept — from Native American society to ancient Mesopotamia, Rome and

---

[16] Ibid., 185.

[17] Hoebel, E. Adamson. *The Cheyennes: Indians of the Great Plains.* New York: Holt, Rinehart and Winston, Case Studies in Cultural Anthropology 1960.

[18] Thomsen, Marie-Louise. "Witchcraft and Magic in Ancient Mesopotamia" in *Witchcraft and Magic in Europe: Biblical and Pagan Societies.* Philadelphia: University of Pennsylvania Press 2001, 79.

Greece. This belief was also present among the tribes of Tierra Del Fuego according to early 20th century ethnologist John Cooper. Cooper noted that malevolent spirits who reside in "forest caves send sickness or death." [19] Likewise, the rituals used to rid the land of the living of these maligned ghosts were similar. It was important to sooth the ill feelings of the ghost, to rectify the wrongs. For some spirits, this was not possible given their characteristics during life. Cooper wrote "The dead are feared, especially witch-doctors, who have power even after their death." [20] One of the Tierra del Fuego tribes, the Yahgans, "believe the soul remains near the grave or wanders over the woods and mountains, especially at night, happy or unhappy, according to moral conduct in life." [21] Other tribes in the area who also feared the ghost of the "witch-doctor," or shaman shared this belief. "The dead know what is taking place on earth," wrote Cooper, "but take no active part in human affairs, except dead witch-doctors." [22] However, the spirits of some of these feared shamans were consulted during times of need because it was believed that they still maintained power over the elements.

Ghosts in other cultural settings even played an important role in a nation's leadership:

"According to a native account," wrote Sir James Frazer, "the origin of the power of Melanesian chiefs lies entirely in the belief that they have communication with mighty ghosts, and wield that supernatural power whereby they can bring the influence of the ghosts to bear." [23]

It was the fear of these ghosts, however, that gave the chief his authority and enforcement abilities. Once the people began to doubt the existence of such authority based in ghostly creatures the chief's ability to rule began to crumble.

In Celtic society people were often buried under trees after they died and it was believed that the tree "embodied the ghost of the

---

[19] Cooper, John M. *Analytical and Critical Bibliography of the Tribes of Tierra del Fuego and Adjacent Territory.* Washington: Smithsonian Institution Bureau of American Ethnology Bulletin 63, 1917, 148.
[20] Ibid 149.
[21] Ibid 151.
[22] Ibid.
[23] Frazer, Sir James. *The Golden Bough: A study in magic and religion.* Hertfordshire: Wordsworth Editions 1993, 84.

person buried under it." [24] However, as MacCulloch wonders, how then did the ghost differentiate itself from a tree spirit? It was MacCulloch's belief that trees became objects of worship because they were believed to be the embodiments of ghosts — not because they were in themselves deities. Likewise fairies may be ghosts of the dead, which is why they have so many of the same characteristics such as appearing as hovering lights, haunting certain tumuli and mid-night dances. MacCulloch wrote, "generally the family ghost has become a brownie, lutin, or pooka, haunting the hearth and doing the household work. Fairy corresponds in all respects to old ancestral ghost, and the one has succeeded to the place of the other, while the fairy is even said to be the ghost of a dead person." [25] MacCulloch footnotes this statement by offering a comparison: "The mischievous brownie who overturns furniture and smashes crockery is an exact reproduction of the Poltergeist." [26]

To MacCulloch and others the ghost is the true fairy and the various nature spirits that have so much influence over individuals world-wide. While this is an attractive theory and one that does explain some of the similarities of the folklore of ghosts and fairies, it does not account for all of them. Many of the stories concerning nature spirits speak of certain "themes" or core elements of how these particular spirits, be they of the water, air, stone, forests or mountains, act. They do not seem to deviate very far from these core elements regardless where they are found around the world. Ghosts, on the other hand, behave either as they did in life or as some representative of an evil underworld god or as souls waiting to be reborn into this world once again. While they may have common attributes of description, they do not have common behaviors.

To MacCulloch the ghosts of the dead were the origins for most of the fertility and nature spirits. "[I]n Scandinavia, they may have been held to have an influence on fertility, as an extension of the belief that certain slain persons represented spirits of fertility, or

---

[24] MacCulloch, J. A. *The Religion of the Ancient Celts.* Mineola: Dover Publications, Inc. 2003, 202.
[25] Ibid 166.
[26] Ibid.

because trees and plants growing on the barrows of the dead were thought to be tenanted by their spirits." [27]

To Native American people this fairy-spirit-ghost tie may also make sense. According to David Whitley, an expert on rock art in the American West, "Throughout far-western North America, whirlwinds were believed to contain ghosts, a particular kind of supernatural spirit." [28] We must use caution however in our assignment of terms. Did/do the Native Americans believe these spirits to be ghosts or were they ghostly spirits? We cannot always assume that we have accurate translations of abstract terms or concepts.

The only physical form that a ghost may take that is visible to the living, at least to the Comanche, is as indicated the whirlwind or "dust devil." According to anthropologist David E. Jones the whirlwind "is the only form by which the ghost will make his presence known during daylight hours. [29]

Whirlwinds in Nishinam tradition denoted the arrival of good spirits to bear the soul of the recently departed to the afterworld. "When an Indian sees one of those little dust-columns which are frequent in this windy climate," wrote Stephen Powers, "he thinks some beatific soul is ascending in it to the Happy Western Land." [30]

The ancient Greeks believed that ghosts and werewolves were closely associated. In fact, an early second century CE tale of Pausanias ("Euthymus of Loci drives a werewolf into the sea") appears to make werewolves a sub-category of ghosts. [31] Contrary to MacCulloch's views, the Greeks felt that a ghost is a supernatural being that may alter its shape but they did not recognize it is a nature spirit.

Most of our fears of ghosts, regardless of where or when we live, come from the belief that they are somehow bad, evil, and

---

[27] Ibid 169.

[28] Whitley, David S. *A Guide to Rock Art Sites: Southern California and Southern Nevada.* Missoula: Mountain Press Publishing Company 1996, 75.

[29] Jones, David E. *Sanapia Comanche Medicine Woman.* New York: Holt, Rinehart and Winston 1972, 65.

[30] Powers, Stephen. *Tribes of California.* Berkeley: University of California Press 1976, 328.

[31] Ogden, Daniel. Magic, Witchcraft, and Ghosts in the Greek and Roman Worlds. Oxford: Oxford University Press 2002, 175.

cause the living to suffer. Do we assume then that ghosts are inherently bad souls? According to 19th century Celtic scholar James Bonwick, "The Irish, like the ancient Jews, held that bad men, especially, could walk this earth after death..."[32]

Rock art from Red Rock Canyon, Nevada with a "whirlwind" symbol.

In Hindu culture, ghosts are also considered the vengeful spirits of the dead. Pregnant women, suicides, those who have been murdered or drowned, those who have been struck by lightning and those who died hating someone are likely candidates to become ghosts. These ghosts are, as one anthropologist writes, "difficult to

---

[32] Bonwick, James. *Irish Druids and Old Irish Religions.* New York: Barnes & Noble Books 1986, 98. A reprint of the 1894 edition.

handle...but some of them have been tamed and are thus in the service of some persons."[33]

However, not all "ghosts" are necessarily bad. To the West African people known as the Ashanti, pregnancy is caused by the mixing of a male spirit with the woman's blood. For the first eight days after delivery, the baby is considered a "ghost child." "It is believed that a ghost mother in the spirit world has lost this child and will make an effort to get it back," wrote anthropologist Elman Service. [34] During these eight days it is unknown if the baby will live or die but upon the eighth day a ceremony is held to formally accept the child as a human child, it is then named and its tribal lineage established.

---

[33] Service, Elman R. *Profiles in Ethnography.* New York: Harper & Row, Publishers 1963, 479.
[34] Ibid 377.

2 Ghostly Activities

In Lakota tradition the human soul is composed of two parts. The *woniya* (breath of life) and *wanagi*, or spirit. When an individual dies both of these go to the spirit land. The spirit may come back to the physical world to visit. After death but before the spirit goes to the spirit land it may attempt to cause harm to its survivors if it was not pleased with them prior to death.

Because the spirit land is so far away many people believe that human spirits "will not come when called. They can not be bought with gifts. They do not care for men who are alive." [35] Others, however, believe that they have seen ghosts. Some Lakota believe that seeing a ghost is not harmful but the Lakota believe that if an individual hears a ghost bad luck will occur. Others though believe that seeing a ghost is very dangerous and commonly causes the observer to suffer a stroke.

To the Comanche this is called "ghost sickness. "The particular horror of the ghost," writes anthropologist David Jones, "is his ability to deform his victims, usually by causing contortions of the facial muscles and in some instances paralysis of hands and feet." [36] Also called "twisted face," the stroke is usually tied directly to the amount of fear produced by the apparition. The ability to control fear is a sure way to avoid the sickness. Ghost sickness usually occurs to individuals who are caught alone outside at night.

Spirits are able to speak with the living but that brings danger to the individual. To hear a ghost in mourning means that a family member will soon die.

The Cheyenne take special care in the proper disposal of the dead to ensure that the spirit will begin its journey to the Milky Way [37] where the spirits reside. Many Native American tribes believe that ghosts like company and will try to take the spirit of a living person

---

[35] Walker, James R. *Lakota Belief and Ritual.* Lincoln: University of Nebraska Press 1991, 72.

[36] Jones, David E. *Sanapia Comanche Medicine Woman.* New York: Holt, Rinehart and Winston 1972, 66.

[37] Many Native American tribes believe that the Milky Way is the final home for the dead.

with them on their journey to the after life. This, of course, may result in the death of another person—especially a child who may be more susceptible to such dangers.

It is the ghost's desire for company that causes many of the ghost sickness cases in Paiute society. Believed to be the second or third major cause of illness among the Paiute, depending on the informant, ghosts attempt to capture the breaths of their relatives, causing them to die, so that they will have more company in the afterworld. Those who are suffering from other forms of illness must be particularly careful in their weakened state since it will be easy for the ghost to capture their breaths. "Ghosting" can also be caused by dreaming of the deceased, which acts to summon the ghost.

Ghost in Navajo tradition live up to their reputation—they are truly frightening! "Ghosts may chase people, jump on them, tug their clothes, or throw dirt upon them," noted anthropologist Clyde Kluckhohn in his book, *The Navaho.* Seeing a ghost is also viewed as a bad omen and certain rituals must be observed to protect the observer and keep his family safe from death. As previously discussed, ghosts are believed to be the malignant part of a dead person which returns to the world of the living to seek revenge and to wreak havoc.

Ghosts cause anti-social behavior in Navajo society by causing people to break taboos, "by telling them to do the opposite of what has been decreed." [38]

The dual aspect of the soul is acknowledged by many native cultures. The Haisla on the Pacific Northwest coast believed that a single entity, called the hziq, was both the soul and the ghost. This hziq was dangerous immediately after death as it could kill others and take their souls. It also could be reincarnated.

This duality was an important distinction of the Kēlta Indians as well. "According to them," wrote Stephen Powers, "there is an evil spirit or devil...and a good spirit; but the good spirit is nameless. The evil spirit is positive, active, and powerful; but the good spirit is negative and passive. The former is without, and ranges through space on evil errands bent; but the latter is within them, it is their

---

[38] Reichard, Gladys A. *Navaho Religion: A Study of Symbolism.* Princeton: Princeton University Press 1950, 589.

own spirit, their better nature, or conscience." [39] At death, the Kēlta believed that a little bird captures the soul and takes it to the spirit-land. However, if the individual was a bad person a hawk swoops down and eats the little bird, soul and all.

The Chinook also believed in a two-soul aspect. According to Chinook tradition, "Each person has two souls, a large one and a small one. When a person falls sick the lesser soul leaves the body. When the conjurers catch it again and return it to him he will recover." [40] However, if the souls becomes too small and no longer fits the body the individual will not recover and will die.

According to anthropologist Marie Mauzé ghosts in Kwakiutl tradition

- "appear just before the death of a person to fetch the soul.
- Ghosts are feared and avoided by the living.
- Their presence near villages can cause bad weather, and their sight is deadly.
- Ghost are visible when they come to fetch the soul of a person before the death.
- If ghosts have the power of taking life away, they also have the power of bringing back the life of someone who has been killed." [41]

Preventative actions were undertaken by the Delaware Indians in 19th century Oklahoma to keep ghosts away from new born and infant children. Afraid that harmful spirits would attempt to steal small children, the children were "wrapped as soon as possible in adult's clothing, by way of this disguise, so that the ghosts would not notice it was new-born. Similarly deer-skin strings or strips of corn husk were tied on the wrists of children so that the ghost would

---

[39] Powers, Stephen. *Tribes of California.* Berkeley: University of California Press 1976, 91.

[40] Hardin, Terri, ed. *Legends & Lore of the American Indians.* New York: Barnes & Noble, Inc. 1993, 422.

[41] Mauzé, Marie. "The Concept of the Person and Reincarnation among the Kwakiutl Indians" in *Amerindian Rebirth: Reincarnation Belief Among North American Indians and Inuit.* Toronto: University of Toronto Press 1990, 190.

think they were tied fast to earth; and holes cut in their little moccasins so that they could not follow the spirit trail." [42]

A spirit or ghost, called the *inipi* was one of the supernatural beings of the Kawaiisu Indians of the Great Basin. This creature may be visible or invisible and, if visible, may appear as a human being. They will often give themselves away by suddenly disappearing, flying away or being unscathed by bullets. They have also been described as having horns (although this may be due to Christian influence) or appearing in the form of a skeleton with red eyes. The inipi is in every human being and animal and is regarded as the essence of life. The inipi may "wander off" during sleep and it also leaves permanently at death.

At death the inipi normally stays nearby and will visit friends and family as well as check up on property owned prior to death. Reportedly the inipi takes acorns and pinions from trees where it had gathered them before death which has resulted in a reduction in the amount of food available for consumption for the village.

Ethnologist Maurice Zigmond noted "At the time of burial someone might enjoin the inipi to go off to its new abode and not do injury to the survivors. As the mourners leave the place of internment, they are careful not to look back lest they catch sight of the ghost—an experience that would of itself be an evil omen." [43]

Eventually the inipi takes a path eastward across the desert to the afterworld. When people walk through the desert and a sudden gust of hot wind blows across their path it is, according to tradition, an inipi passing by. For the most part the inipi act as they did while living and may tease the survivors and play tricks on them. However, anyone who was unkind to the individual prior to death may be haunted in a frightening manner.

Inipi have hidden or thrown about animal traps, have knocked on the outside of homes, have walked around houses after dark (their steps were heard but no one was seen), cough loudly, pull covers off of sleeping people, throw pans and utensils on the floor and whistle.

---

[42] Harrington, M. R. "A Preliminary Sketch of Lenape Culture. *American Anthropologist,* Vol. 15, No. 2, 1913, pg. 212.

[43] Zigmond, Maurice. "The Supernatural World of the Kawaiisu" in *Flowers of the Wind: Papers on Ritual and Symbolism in California and the Southwest.* Ed. by Thomas C. Blackburn. Socorro: Ballena Press, pp. 59-95.

Inipi may also be in the control of evil shaman who freely sends it out on destructive missions. Supposedly inipi under a shaman's power have pushed men off a cliff and caused cars to crash. Whirlwinds, as indicated previously, are almost always believed to be spirits and inipi. They should always be avoided as at times they attempt to enter the body through the mouth which results in death.

Because inipi fear tobacco and the smoke of blue sage, these are useful to keep ghosts away. Certain charms are also useful in this way, including two bird wings attached to a stick and a spiral made from strips of wood. They are hung from the ceiling and freely move in air currents.

3 Ceremonies of Appeasement

Ceremony and ritual is of utmost importance to traditional Native Americans. Specific ceremonies and rituals have been created and performed for a variety of reasons—including the manipulation of weather, to ensure a successful hunt, to offer protection, to ease childbirth and to control the spirits. Some of the more important ceremonies are performed to ease the souls of the dead into the afterworld and to protect the tribe from ghosts and other malevolent spirits.

The following account is by Dr. S. G. Wright, acting physician to the Leech Lake Agency, Minnesota and illustrates the importance of ceremonies and offerings surrounding burials:

> "Pagan Indians or those who have not become Christians still adhere to the ancient practice of feasting at the grave of departed friends; the object is to feast with the departed; that is, they believe that while they partake of the visible material the departed spirit partakes at the same time of the spirit that dwells in the food. From ancient time it was customary to bury with the dead various articles, such especially as were most valued in lifetime. The idea was that there was a spirit dwelling in the article represented by the material article; thus the war-club contained a spiritual war-club, the pipe a spiritual pipe, which could be used by the departed in another world. These several spiritual implements were supposed, of course, to accompany the soul, to be used also on the way to its final abode. This habit has now ceased." [44]

Like many indigenous societies, the Mono Indians living in the Owens Valley area of eastern California observed annual mourning ceremonies to remember those of their ranks who had died during

---

[44] Yarrow, H.C. "A further contribution to the study of the mortuary customs of the North American Indians," *First Annual Report of the Bureau of Ethnology to the Secretary of the Smithsonian Institution*, Government Printing Office, Washington, 1881, pages 87-204.

the prior year. The mourning ceremony may have originated in the south among the Luiseño and Gabrielino tribes because, Kroeber wrote, "the anniversary received its principal development among the same people that chiefly shaped the Jimson-weed cult." In addition, Kroeber stated, "it is even possible that the two sets of rites flowed northward in conjunction, and that the anniversary outreached its mate because the absence of the Jimson-weed plant north of the Yokuts checked the invasion of the rites based upon it."[45]

While the Jimson-weed cult was an important aspect of shamanism in California, it is doubtful that the mourning ceremony was a direct result of it. Death observances are universal among Native American groups and while cultural sharing did take place it cannot be shown that the two rites have a direct correlation to a specific point of origin.

The mourning ceremony took place in the fall to mark the end of the year of mourning, much like Samhain was a pivotal time for the Celts to mark the turning of the year and to remember the dead. Relatives of the deceased were required to abstain from meat and grease, [46] could not wash and were to avoid any festivities. The mourning ceremony itself was an act to symbolically wash away the grief of relatives and, most importantly, to "contribute somewhat to the cohesion of the band members." [47]

Following the ceremony, the deceased person's house and bedding was burned, a man's favorite horse was killed and left by the grave site, the manes and tails of his other horses were cut. The personal property of the deceased was buried with the body and, according to some informants, food and presents were put in the grave with up to $50 worth of articles purchased specifically for the occasion. .

---

[45] Krober, A. L. "Elements of Culture in Native California" in *The California Indians*, ed. by R. F. Heizer and M.A. Whipple. Berkeley: University of California Press 1971, 48.

[46] Whiting stated however that there were no food taboos observed by the Harney Valley Paiute.

[47] Steward, Julian H. "Basin-Plateau Aboriginal Sociopolitical Groups" in *Bureau of American Ethnology Bulletin 120*. Washington: Smithsonian Institution 1938, 55.

Close relatives cut their hair short, as was the custom among many Native American tribes, the closer the relationship the shorter their hair. Women would slash their arms and legs with a knife and dump red paint over their heads as signs of grief. Sarah Winnemucca recounted how her people mourned their dead:

"They cut off their hair, and also cut long gashes in their arms and legs, and they were all bleeding as if they would die with the loss of blood. This continued for several days, for this is the way we mourn our dead. When the woman's husband dies, she is first to cut off her hair, and then she braids it and puts it across his breast; then his mother and sisters, his father and brothers and all his kinsfolk cut their hair. The widow is to remain unmarried until her hair is the same length as before..." [48]

The dead were usually buried in the knee-chest position but some evidently were buried flat on their backs. The community, except children, participated in covering the body with stones. Children were prohibited from being near the deceased or participating in the mourning ceremony. Those killed in battle, unless they died near the village, were abandoned where they fell. Mothers who died in childbirth were buried with the infant in their arms and infants who died were buried in their cradles.

"It is considered dangerous," Whiting noted, "to visit graves or to think of or mention the name of the dead. Such thoughts might bring the ghost of the deceased, who would snatch the breath of his loved ones whom he had left behind." [49]

Mourning ceremonies were led by the chief and other surrounding tribes and villages were invited, normally twelve days in advance of the event. Mourning ceremonies were irregular among the Owens Valley Mono and not always during the fall months. According to Spier this was due to "the frequency...linked to deaths and the affluence of the mourning families, who paid most of the costs." [50]

---

[48] Hopkins, Sarah Winnemucca. *Life Among the Piutes.* Reno: University of Nevada Press 1994, 21.

[49] Whiting, Beatrice Blyth. *Paiute Sorcery.* New York: Viking Fund Publications in Anthropology, Number 15, 1950, 107.

[50] Spier, op cit. 434.

Mourning ceremonies had an intricate pattern to them and included many of the things that many Native American festivities had. Paid singers, shamanic contests, parades of participants and ritualized bathing frequently occurred. In the 1870s, the Cry Ceremony was introduced to the Paiutes and within twenty years it had become the most pervasive ceremony among the Owens Valley and Southern Paiutes. The Crying Ceremony took place over two nights immediately after a death and before the funeral and was repeated as a memorial one or two years later. During the ceremony song cycles known as Bird Songs and Salt Songs were sung by two groups of singers. Between the cycles, emotional speeches were given and the deceased belongings were given away. This ceremony remained as an important ritual into the twentieth century.

Mourning ceremonies among the Eastern Mono and all other Northern Paiute groups lasted seven days. Images of the deceased were made by relatives and were burned with personal property of the dead. Usually the burning was done at or near the grave sites where huts or holes were made for offerings. There is some disagreement among ethnologists as to how the dead were desposed of. Some, including Spier, Wilkie and Lawton, wrote that burial was the principal means of disposal while others, including Gould, stated that the body was buried under rocks. Aginsky wrote that cremation was the general method of disposal. Relatives, corpse handlers and singers were mentioned most frequently as the people who dug the graves. Corpse handlers and singers were paid for their services. The differences in corpse disposal have not been discussed but it may have been due to differing geographic locations and the difficulty of digging in the soil or the amount of time that was available. "Death baskets," used to collect the cremated bones, were possibly used to rebury the remains after a period of time.

The Chumash Indians along the Santa Barbara coast performed the following ritual as observed by Pedro Fages, Military Governor of Alta California from 1770 to 1774:

"When any Indian dies, they carry the body to the adoratory, or place near the village dedicated to their idols. There they celebrate the mortuary ceremony, and watch all the following night, some of them gathered about a huge fire until daybreak; then come all the rest (men and women), and four of them begin the ceremony in this wise. One Indian, smoking tobacco in a large stone pipe, goes first; he is followed by the other three, all passing thrice around the body; but each time he passes the head, his companions lift the skin with which it is covered, that the priest may blow upon it three mouthfuls of smoke. On arriving at the feet, they all four together stop to sing I know not what laudation. Then come the near and remote relatives of the deceased, each one giving to the chief celebrant a string of beads, something over a span in length. Then immediately there is raised a sorrowful outcry and lamentation from all the mourners. When this sort of solemn response is ended, the four ministers take up the body, and all the Indians follow them, singing, to the cemetery which they have prepared for the purpose, where it is given sepulture; with the body are buried some little things made by the deceased person himself; some other objects are deposited round about the spot where the body rests, and over it, thrust into the earth, is raised a spear or very long rod, painted in various colors. At the foot of this rod are left a few relics, which naturally represent the ability and kind occupation which the man had while he was living. If the deceased is a woman, they leave strung on the rod some of the boxes and baskets which she was accustomed to weave." [51]

The Eastern and Southeastern Pomo who live in the northern coast range of California approximately 100 miles north of San Francisco participated in a "ghost ceremony." This ceremony, according to anthropologists, was tied to the intense feelings of the Pomo around death and involved the impersonation of the dead by specially trained actors.

There were three participants in the Pomo ghost ceremony. They were the "ghosts," the "ash ghosts" who know how to handle live coals without harm, and the "initiates" who know the rules of the ceremony and dances.

---

[51] Priestly, H. I. *A Historical, Political and Natural Description of California, by Pedro Fages*. Berkeley: University of California Press 1937, pgs 31-36, 47-53.

"The first night," wrote McLendon and Lowy, two anthropologists who have studied the Pomo, "the ghosts made their presence known by fires in the hills surrounding the village and the thunderlike sounds of dancing in the subterranean Márakh, plus occasional glimpses of flaming figures." [52] These figures are the ghosts of those cremated which is why they have a special relationship to fire.

Pomo girl, photo taken by Edward S. Curtis between 1907 and 1922.

---

[52] McLendon, Sally and Michael J. Lowy. "Eastern Pomo and Southeastern Pomo" in *Handbook of North American Indians, Vol. 8: California.* Washington: Smithsonian Institute 1978, 316.

The next morning the ceremonial leader, or "captain" called the ghosts which appeared, some in flames. The ghost appeared from the four cardinal directions. They were urged to run for the health of the village and the tribal members. One of the ghosts was identified as that of a recently deceased man. This ghost was "caught" and laid down on the ground. The relatives of the deceased man were instructed to line up on both sides of the entranceway of the subterranean Márakh. The "body" of the ghost was decorated with a profusion of beads by his mourning female relatives. The ghost was then taken into the Márakh or ghost house and all of the males in the village then entered the house as well.

At this time, the women prepared pinole and acorn mush which was placed in front of the house and offered to visitors. The food was eventually divided so that everyone could participate in an impromptu feast.

As evening approached fires were seen in the hills and thunder began. As the sun rose the next mourning the sounds changed and the "fire dance" commenced. The ash ghost appeared to handle burning coals and he would eat the hot coals. Over the next day the ghosts were summoned several times, games were played and dancing took place. This was also the time to initiate boys into tribal membership.

According to eye-witness accounts, "the ghosts behaved in certain prescribed ways. They always talked in a special language, using Eastern Pomo lexical items and grammar, but always talking in terms of antonyms and opposites...The ghosts were, on one hand, deliberately mirth-provoking in their behavior, trying to induce the participants to laugh, on the other hand, irascible, easily irritated into terrifying, fire-throwing anger. [53]

The Huron Indians of Canada participated in a mourning ceremony called the Feast of the Dead. This feast was undertaken approximately every 8 to 12 years when all burials were disinterred. Described as a religious ceremony it was also a social event to unify the tribe by re-interring the dead in a common grave.

According to Conrad Heidenreich, upon announcement of the feast date, "each family would get the bodies of their deceased relatives from the keepers of the graves. All except those who had

---

[53] Ibid.

died recently were cleansed of all flesh, which was burned." [54] The intact bodies were placed on litters while the bones of the others were wrapped in robes and carried to the village were the feast was to be held. A large pit up to twenty feet in diameter was dug and the intact bodies were placed on the bottom of the robe lined pit. Those that were only bones were tossed, along with grave goods, into the pit by the family. Once the remains were all in the pit it was covered up with mats, bark and sand. Some of the grave goods were broken to release the souls of the item so that the spirits of the deceased could utilize the item in the afterworld. The Feast of the Dead was very important as it was a traditional way to release the souls for rebirth and to send them on to the afterlife.

One witness to the Huron feast was Jesuit missionary P. de Brebeuf whose account was recorded in 1860:

"...at the village of Ossosane, before the dispersion of the Hurons, ...the ceremony took place in the presence of 2,000 Indians, who offered 1,300 presents at the common tomb, in testimony of their grief. The people belonging to five large villages deposited the bones of their dead in a gigantic shroud, composed of forty-eight robes, each robe being made of ten beaver skins. After being carefully wrapped in this shroud, they were placed between moss and bark. A wall of stones was built around this vast ossuary to preserve it from profanation. Before covering the bones with earth a few grains of Indian corn were thrown by the women upon the sacred relics. According to the superstitious belief of the Hurons the souls of the dead remain near the bodies until the "feast of the dead"; after which ceremony they become free, and can at once depart for the land of spirits, which they believe to be situated in the regions of the setting sun."

An entirely different sort of mourning ceremony was observed by the Halchidhoma, one of the five Yuman tribe residing along the Gila River. The Halchidhoma ceremony was similar to others observed in Southern California and the lower Colorado region. It

---

[54] Heidenreich, Conrad E. "Huron" in *Handbook of North American Indians, Vol. 15: Northeast.* Washington: Smithsonian Institution 1978, 374.

consisted of the burning of an effigy symbolic of the dead and of "sham combat." Called *kĕRu'kåm,* the ceremony appears to have been observed only for men and was an act of remembrance. The *kĕRu'kåm* was normally observed one time on the anniversary of the individual's death.

Once the appointed day and time had been announced to neighboring villages, the image was prepared. Four men were chosen to make the image. The men bathed every morning before the work commenced which was completed deliberately and slowly. The image was made of rags and was intended to look exactly like the deceased and the head and neck were constructed so that the head could move from side to side.

A willow structure was built as was a "meeting shade." The structure was constructed of willow branches and was intended to house those who were going to participate as enemy combatants. The meeting shade was built to accommodate the deceased family. Each structure took four days to finish with the shade completed the day of the ceremony.

Four columns of mourners arrived at the ceremonial site simultaneously and burst out in weeping. Speakers from the four directions addressed the crowd and then the image was erected on a post. As it was carried it was made to move from side to side in time to the words of the speakers. While some cried, others would dance or sing. After the image was erected the two opposing combatant groups, both armed, would engage each other. The one group would pretend to battle to escape their "confinement" while the other group would fight to keep them prisoner. When the image was finally set alight both groups would break their bows and arrows and toss them into the flames. Women would then run around the site, tossing food from baskets at the other mourners. When the baskets were empty they were placed on the woodpile to be burned. Both structures were also burnt at this time.

"When the woodpile was half burned down," Spier related, "all left except for the mourners. The speaker then told them to bear up under their loss, speaking as though the death had just occurred. He then left. The man who tended the cremation also tended this burning. He handled the image carefully as though it were the corpse. He saw that it was wholly consumed, divided the ashes into four parts, and buried them in four holes. Then the mourners left.

"Those who made the image and those who took part in the sham fight had to observe the precautions of purification for four days, abstaining from salt, etc., just as at a death." [55]

This ceremony is believed to have ceased around 1847.

The Hopi-Tewa death ceremonies were performed to prepare the deceased for the transition between existences and rebirth. To the Tewa natural birth was regarded as simply a transition from this life to that of another through rebirth. As part of the death ceremony, the body is washed and it was believed to be extremely important for the hair to be washed. An ear of corn was used for this purpose. A cotton mask is placed over the face with a feather tied to it. Feathers were also tied over the head. The face is then partially painted black. These activities make the body light like a cloud, and, according to Michael Stanislawski, "give breath for the otherworld."[56] After this, the deceased receives a new name as it is considered a baby in the afterworld. The body is buried with piki bread and water placed near it with more pottery containers of water nearby. In addition, prayer sticks and a planting stick are placed on the burial mound to serve the soul in the Otherworld. After four days, the soul is believed to depart this world for the next.

Similar burial observances are practiced by the Kickapoo. Grave goods consist of tobacco, a bowl of food and also a wooden spoon which is particularly important as a cultural item. Anyone buried without a wooden spoon must eat foam throughout eternity. After death children under 12 are removed and hidden to protect them from ghost who desire to take others with them to the afterworld. The body is carefully dressed and painted and taken to the burial site by four selected men. One a few chosen tribal members are allowed to witness the burial. Between four days and four years later, another ceremony is conducted, referred to as a ceremonial adoption. The ceremony is held at night to allow the spirit of the deceased to enter the home and partake of a feast. An individual of the same sex and age of the deceased is chosen to become the

---

[55] Spier, Leslie. *Yuman Tribes of the Gila River.* New York: Dover Publications, Inc. 1978, 308.

[56] Stanislawski, Michael B. "Hopi-Tewa" in *Handbook of North American Indians, Vol. 9: Southwest.* Washington: Smithsonian Institute 1978, 599.

"replacement" of the person, thus the adoptee. Gifts are distributed and the adoptee received new clothing.

Yuman Indians, from "United States and Mexican Boundary Survey. Report of William H. Emory..." Washington. 1857

In the Northeastern region of the United States burial ceremonialism became very important at least by the third millennium BCE. Red ochre powder was sprinkled over the body reminiscent of ancient ceremonies going back more than 80,000 years around the world. Elaborate grave goods, including projectile points, stone tools, bone harpoons, needles and awls and a variety of copper items such as bracelets, points and beads were interred with the body. Ground stone amulets and charms have also been found. Magnificent ground slate "bayonets" and spear-points were crafted specifically as grave goods and, at times, were ritually broken or "killed" to release the spirit of the stone. Such elaborate ceremonies and offerings were undertaken to pay respect to the dead and to ensure that the soul would be happy in the Otherworld. This was also undoubtedly a way to ensure that the soul would not return to the land of the living as a ghost to cause harm.

The practice of placing broken goods with the burial is a very old one in North America. An archaeological excavation in San Diego dated to 7370 BCE exposed two burials which had broken metates, also referred to as milling stones, placed over the skulls. [57] Metates were used in food preparation and would have been an important object in the afterlife.

While most ceremonies and rituals concerned with death and burial were performed to ease the soul into the afterlife and to limit the possibility that the soul would return as a ghost, some of the rituals were actually created to destroy the soul of an enemy entirely. The Cherokee "Magic Formula to Destroy Life" is one of these:

"Listen! Now I have come to step over your soul. You are of the wolf clan. Your name is Áyûiuni. Your spittle I have put at rest under he earth.

"I have come to cover you over with the black cloth. I have come to cover you with the black slabs, never to reappear. Toward the black coffin of the upland in the Darkening Land your paths shall stretch out. So shall it be for you.

"The clay of the upland has come to cover you. Instantly the black clay has lodged there where it is at rest at the black

---

[57] Shumway, George, et al. "Scripps Estate Site, San Diego, California: A La Jolla Site Dated 5460 to 7370 Years Before the Present." New York: Annals of the New York Academy of Sciences, Vol. 93, Article 3, Pages 37-132. December 4, 1961.

houses in the Darkening Land. With the black coffin and the black slabs I have come to cover you.

"Now your soul has faded away. It has become blue. When darkness comes your spirit shall grow less and dwindle away, never to reappear. Listen!" [58]

Early ethnographic reports indicate that sacrifice was common in the inhumation practices of several Native tribes. The Apache killed the favorite horse of the deceased, usually by stabbing it in the throat. This to provide the spirit with his horse in death. Animal sacrifice included horses and dogs—the two favored animals. "Most of a man's dogs were killed at his death" wrote Roland Dixon about the Northern Maidu of California. [59]

According to Yarrow, writing about the Otoe Indians of Nebraska, "A pony, first designated by the dying Indian, is led aside and strangled by men hanging to either end of a rope. Sometimes, but not always, a dog is likewise strangled, the heads of both animals being subsequently laid upon the Indian's grave." In fact most tribes in the United States killed a horse or dog as a sacrifice to the spirit and the supernatural.

However, there are disturbing accounts of human sacrifice as well in other parts of the country. One such rather sensational account was given by Yarrow. Contrary to Yarrow's statement below, this particular incident has not been verified:

"An apparently well-authenticated case of attempted burial sacrifice is described by Miss A. J. Allen, and refers to the Wascopums, of Oregon.

At length, by meaning looks and gestures rather than words, it was found that the chief had determined that the deceased boy's friend, who had been his companion in hunting the rabbit, snaring the pheasant, and fishing in the streams, was to be his companion to the spirit land; his son should not be deprived of his associate in the strange world to which he

---

[58] Mooney, James. "The Sacred Formulas of the Cherokees," in *Bureau of American Ethnology, 7th Annual Report, 1885-86.* Washington, 391.
[59] Dixon, Roland B. "The Northern Maidu," *Bulletin of the American Museum of Natural History* (1905), 17:119-346.

had gone; that associate should perish by the hand of his father, and be conveyed with him to the dead-house. This receptacle was built on a long, black rock in the center of the Columbia River, around which, being so near the falls, the current was amazingly rapid. It was thirty feet in length, and perhaps half that in breadth, completely enclosed and sodded except at one end, where was a narrow aperture just sufficient to carry a corpse through. The council overruled, and little George, instead of being slain, was conveyed living to the dead-house about sunset. The dead were piled on each side, leaving a narrow aisle between, and on one of these was placed the deceased boy; and, bound tightly till the purple, quivering flesh puffed above the strong bark cords, that he might die very soon, the living was placed by his side, his face to his till the very lips met, and extending along limb to limb and foot to foot, and nestled down into his couch of rottenness, to impede his breathing as far as possible and smother his cries." [60]

Human sacrifice did occur along the Northwest Coast, the Southeast and, of course, in Meso-America. Such sacrifices were reserved for the deaths of important persons. Those sacrificed may have been slaves, prisoners, servants, a child offered by a civic-minded individual, or the deceased's widow. The majority of "sacrifices," however, were the "killing" of the grave goods, the breaking of clay pots and milling stones, the bending of metal items, the destruction of items intended to accompany the spirit to the afterworld. As stated previously this was done for two reasons. First, such destructive acts freed the spirits of the items so that they would "live" again with the soul and, two, this made the objects worthless to anyone who thought to steal them.

There were certain ways as well to drive ghosts away from the living. The Navajo used white clay, as an opposite to the darkness of the night, to provide protection from ghosts; likewise pollen was spread over the body at the points where a ghost would most likely

---

[60] Yarrow, H.C. "A further contribution to the study of the mortuary customs of the North American Indians," *First Annual Report of the Bureau of Ethnology to the Secretary of the Smithsonian Institution*, Government Printing Office, Washington, 1881, pages 87-204

enter such as the fingertips, ears, hair, etc. Ceremonial drumming was also a powerful exorcism ritual. According to Reichard, "The ghost of the Ancient People was killed by beating the pot drum, for when the Navaho beat it, they beat the face of the enemy." [61]

---

[61] Reichard, Gladys A. *Navaho Religion: A Study of Symbolism.* Princeton: Princeton University Press 1950, 551.

4 Disposition of the Dead

There were several ways in which the bodies of the deceased were disposed of in Native American society. The "proper way" was necessary for the spirit to continue on to the afterworld. To the Colorado River Yumans the only acceptable way was cremation. According to Spier, "Those who were not cremated could not enter the land of the dead." The reason behind this, according to Yuman tradition, is that those who are buried "smell too badly." Unless cremated the soul must live on the north side of the afterworld and must forever wander around carrying boxes or coffins on their heads looking for shady places to rest. "When they tire," an informant states, "they lay them down and sit on them. The dead think this appalling."[62]

Cremation was viewed as a way to release the soul so that it could journey on to the afterworld. "They believe, like all others," wrote Stephen Powers, "that the soul can be disembodied and set free by the agency of fire alone; hence the necessity of burning...when a person of a goodly fatness is burning," he adds, "and his flesh sputters and pops n the flames, the spectators shout the loudest, believing that his spirit is enjoying a happy release."[63]

The Pomo and Northern Paiute cremated their dead, at least prior to their Caucasian domination. By the late 1880's the customs of the Pomo had been so influenced by Christianity that the only tribal members cremated were "those killed or hanged by the whites."[64] The rest were buried. The Northern Paiute usually reserved cremation for those suspected of witchcraft and buried the others in rock crevices, caves, rockshelters or on hillsides. The Western Shoshone used various means to dispose of the dead, including cremation by burning the house down with the body inside, burial in rock-slides, talus slopes, caves and rockshelters or

---

[62] Spier, Leslie. *Yuman Tribes of the Gila River.* New York: Dover Publications, Inc. 1978, 299.

[63] Powers, Stephen. *Tribes of California.* Berkeley: University of California Press 1976, 207-208.

[64] Ibid., 153.

in soft soil. They also would simply abandon the body inside the deceased's home or simply outside covered with brush.

Unlike the Pomo and Paiute, the Karok, however, "profess abhorrence for incremation" and bury their dead near their residences so that their friends and relatives can watch over the gravesite and protect. When Stephen Powers conducted his research in the late 1800's most Karok gravesites had white picket fences erected around them in imitation of American custom, although this may have been a modified version of the pen burial which was common in other parts of the country.

Among the Northwest coastal tribes, cremation was rare but was practiced for tribal members who died away from home—their ashes sometimes brought home in baskets. Burial practices varied from tribe to tribe with extended burials in deep graves which were then topped with stones done by the Wailaki or in a flexed position wrapped in blankets as done by the Lassik.

The Shasta Indians also reserved cremation for those who died away from home. Their ashes were also collected and carried home for burial. The Shasta owned family burial plots and either buried the deceased personal belongings with the body or burned them.

The Achumawi, also known as the Pitt River Indians, quickly disposed of the dead by cremation without any ceremony or purification ceremony. The belongings of the dead were also burned and survivors were forbidden from speaking the deceased's name, [65] for "his soul had gone to the western mountains and no one wanted to give it an excuse to return, since the soul does not want to travel alone and might return to get a traveling companion from among those most dear to it." [66]

The dead were so feared by the Achumawi that no one dared to ask what happened to the soul after it had gone on to the western mountains.

According to Stephen Powers, the Wappo Indians, living in the Calistoga Hot Springs area of Northern California, "immediately incinerated (the dead), and the ashes flung into the air. They believe that the spirit is thus born aloft and flies away to a grotto

---

[65] This avoidance was commonly observed by Native Americans.

[66] Olmsted, D.L. and Omer C. Stewart. "Achumawi" in *Handbook of North American Indians, Vol. 8: California.* Washington: Smithsonian Institute 1978,232.

hard by the sea at Punta de los Reyes. In this grotto is a fire which burns without ceasing, and which no living being may behold without being instantly stricken blind. The disembodied spirit enters, hovers over and around this fire for a season, then flutters forth again and wings its flight over the ocean to the Happy Western Land." [67]

The Indians living along the Hudson River buried their dead "in their finest garb in a grave lined with boughs." Reportedly, the body was covered with clay and earth and stones were piled atop the burial to a height of seven to eight feet. The grave was then surrounded with a "palisade." There is some dispute as to the position of the body with some stating that it was laid out flat and others that the body was placed in a sitting position "upon a stone or block of wood as if the body were sitting upon a stool." [68] Grave good such as utensils and provisions were buried with the body to accompany the spirit to the afterworld.

Lockett wrote that when an adult Hopi dies "the nearest relatives by blood wash the head, tie a feather offering to the hair so that it will hang over the forehead, wrap the body in a good robe and carry it to one of the graveyards which are in the valleys near the mesas. The body is buried in a sitting position so that it faces east. This is done within a few hours after death has occurred. The third night, a bowl containing some food, a prayer-stick offering, and a feather and string, are carried to the grave. The string is placed so that it points from the grave to the west. The next morning, the fourth, the soul is supposed to rise from the grave and proceed in the direction indicated by the string, where it enters the 'skeleton house.' This is believed to be situated somewhere near the Canyon of the Colorado.

"Any bodies of young children who have not yet been initiated into any fraternity are not buried in the ground, but in a crevice of rock somewhere near the mother's home and covered with stones. A string is left hanging out, pointing to the home of the family. The spirit of the child is believed to return and to be re-born in the next

[67] Powers, Op cit., 200.
[68] Campisi, Jack. "The Hudson Valley Indians Through Dutch Eyes" in *Neighbors and Intruders: An Ethnohistorical Exploration of the Indians of Hudson's River*. Ottawa: Canadian Ethnology Service Paper No. 39, National Museum of Man Mercury Series 1976, 176.

child born in the family, or to linger about till the mother dies and then to go with her to the underworld." [69]

The most unusual form of disposal of the dead was observed by the Paiute residing in the northeastern part of California in what is now Modoc County. Here the dead were placed in hot springs. [70]

Similar burials in hot springs were reported by Captain J.H. Simpson:

> "Skull Valley, which is a part of the Great Salt Lake Desert, and which we have crossed to-day, Mr. George W. Bean, my guide over this route last fall, says derives its name from the number of skulls which have been found in it, and which have arisen from the custom of the Goshute Indians burying their dead in springs, which they sank with stones or keep down with sticks. He says he has actually seen the Indians bury their dead in this way near the town of Provo, where he resides." [71]

Yarrow noted "This peculiar mode of burial is entirely unique, so far as known, and but from the well-known probity of the relator might well be questioned, especially when it is remembered that in the country spoken of water is quite scarce and Indians are careful not to pollute the streams or springs near which they live. Conjecture seems useless to establish a reason for this disposition of the dead, unless we are inclined to attribute it to the natural indolence of the savage, or a desire to poison the springs for white persons." [72]

However, the use of hot springs as drinking water is doubtful and the fact that Paiute groups in Northern California also buried their

---

[69] Lockett, Hattie Greene. "The Unwritten Literature of the Hopi," *Social Science Bulletin Number 2, Vol. IV, Number 4*, May 15, 1933. Tucson: University of Arizona

[70] Heizer, Robert F. and Adan E. Treganza. *Mines and Quarries of the Indians of California.* Ramona: Ballena Press 1972, 296.

[71] Yarrow, H.C. "A further contribution to the study of the mortuary customs of the North American Indians," *First Annual Report of the Bureau of Ethnology to the Secretary of the Smithsonian Institution*, Government Printing Office, Washington, 1881, pages 87-204.

[72] Ibid.

dead at times in hot springs would indicate that it was more a custom than a form of hostility against the encroaching whites.

Other water-oriented burials include canoe burials by the Massasauga Indians who resided along the north shore of Lake Ontario and rarely by the Chumash who live in the Santa Barbara, California area. The bodies were placed in the canoe and buried in the ground and not actually placed in the water. The Chumash example is thought to be that of a renowned fisherman. There are anecdotal accounts of infants being set adrift in mourning cradles such as described by George Catlin in his 1844 *History of North American Indians* of Chinook customs:

"This little cradle has a strap which passes over the woman's forehead whilst the cradle rides on her back, and if the child dies during its subjection to this rigid mode, its cradle becomes its coffin, forming a little canoe, in which it lies floating on the water in some sacred pool, where they are often in the habit of fastening their canoes containing the dead bodies of the old and young, or, which in often the case, elevated into the branches of trees, where their bodies are left to decay and their bones to dry whilst they are bandaged in many skins and curiously packed in their canoes, with paddles to propel and ladles to bale them out, and provisions to last and pipes to smoke as they are performing their "long journey after death to their contemplated hunting grounds,' which these people think is to be performed in their canoes."

The Chinook canoes intended for adults were carefully and beautifully made for the deceased. Henry Schoolcraft wrote in 1857 of the efforts taken by the Chinook to produce these burial canoes:

"These canoes are carved out of a single log of cedar, and are of the most beautiful proportions. Some are of a size capable of holding a hundred persons, with all their arms and accouterments. The canoe in question was about thirty-five feet long. It was first thoroughly washed; then two large, square holes were cut through the bottom, probably for the two-fold purpose of letting out any water that might collect in the canoe during rain storms, and also to prevent the canoe from ever again being used. Nice new mats of rushes were then placed inside, and on these the corpse, wrapped in new blankets, was laid."[73]

Along with the body, the personal possessions of the deceased were also placed into the canoe to be used in the afterlife. Many of the items were intentionally broken or pierced in order to release the spirit of the object and to make them worthless if stolen.

19th century illustration of a Chinook mourning cradle being set adrift.

The year following internment in the canoe the bones were gathered and removed "and, after being wrapped in new white

---

[73] Schoolcraft, Henry Rowe. *History of the Indian Tribes of the United States.* Philadelphia: J.B. Lippincott & Co. 1857, 621.

cotton cloth, are enclosed in a box and buried in the earth, usually under the canoe; but, in some instances, they are gathered into a sort of family burying ground." [74]

This gathering of the bones was a private ceremony, forbidden for others to see as "the dead were standing around to see the ceremony, and would be angry if a stranger was there."[75]

Canoe Burial

Indians of Oregon and Washington also used canoe burials as a common mode of disposal. The canoes, however, were not set adrift in waterways but placed above ground in tree forks or on posts. Yarrow noted in his 1881 study:

---

[74] Ibid., 622.
[75] Ibid.

"Upon the Columbia River the Tsinūk had in particular two very noted cemeteries, a high isolated bluff about three miles below the mouth of the Cowlitz, called Mount Coffin, and one some distance above, called Coffin Rock. The former would appear not to have been very ancient. Mr. Broughton, one of Vancouver's lieutenants, who explored the river, makes mention only of *several* canoes at this place; and Lewis and Clarke, who noticed the mount, do not speak of them at all, but at the time of Captain Wilkes's expedition it is conjectured that there were at least 3,000. A fire caused by the carelessness of one of his party destroyed the whole, to the great indignation of the Indians."[76]

British Columbian Canoe Burial

"Box burials" were common in the Northwest and among the Eskimo. Most of these box containers were decorated with exquisite art work. According to noted 19th century historian Hubert H. Bancroft:

"The Eskimos do not as a rule bury their dead, but double the body up and place it on the side in a plank box which is

---

[76] Yarrow, op cit.

elevated three or four feet from the ground and supported by four posts. The grave-box is often covered with painted figures of 156 birds, fishes and animals. Sometimes it is wrapped in skins placed upon an elevated frame and covered with planks or trunks of trees so as to protect it from wild beasts. Upon the frame, or in the grave box are deposited the arms, clothing, and sometimes the domestic utensils of the deceased. Frequent mention is made by travelers of burial places where the bodies lie exposed with their heads placed towards the north."[77]

In many arctic areas where the ground is covered in ice and raw materials are absent the dead are simply left on the ground and covered with stones or devoured by dogs and wolves.

Other tribes in arctic also used boxes, such as the Kalosh. However, contrary to the Eskimo that placed the entire body in the box, the Kalosh cremated their dead and placed the ashes in the container. "Their grave boxes or tombs are interesting," wrote Frederic Whymper in his 1870 account. "They contain only the ashes of the dead. These people invariably burn the deceased. On one of the boxes I saw a number of faces painted, long tresses of human hair depending therefrom. Each head represented a victim of the (happily) deceased one's ferocity. In his day he was doubtless more esteemed than if he had never harmed a fly. All their graves are much ornamented with carved and painted faces and other devices."

The illustration below depicts one of these interesting burial containers used by the Innuit.

---

[77] Bancroft, Hubert H. Nat. Races of Pac. States, 1874 vol. i, p. 69.

A variation of the box burial is the "house burial." Yarrow wrote of these structures created for the deceased:

"The grave is dug after the style of the whites and the coffin then placed in it. After it has been covered it is customary though not universal, to build some kind of an inclosure over it or around it in the shape of a small house, shed, lodge or fence. These are from 2 to 12 feet high, from 2 to 6 feet wide, and from 5 to 12 feet long. Some of these are so well inclosed that it is impossible to see within and some are quite open. Occasionally a window is placed in the front side. Sometimes these enclosures are covered with cloth, which is generally white, sometimes partly covered, and some have none. Around the grave, both outside and inside of the inclosure, various articles are placed, as guns, canoes, dishes, pails, cloth, sheets, blankets, beads, tubs, lamps, bows, mats, and occasionally a roughly-carved human image rudely painted. It is said that around and in the grave of one Clallam chief, buried a few years ago, $500 worth of such things were left. Most of these articles are cut or broken so as to render them valueless to man and to prevent their being stolen. Poles are also often erected, from 10 to 30 feet long, on which American flags, handkerchiefs, clothes, and cloths of various colors are hung. A few graves have nothing of this kind. On some graves these things are renewed every year or two. This depends mainly on the number of relatives living and the esteem in which they hold the deceased."

House burial

This form of burial was most often utilized in the east. "House burials" however included the internment of the body under house structures in continuous use by the living. An archaeological excavation in a Woodland culture site in Somerset County, Pennsylvania uncovered 10 burials inside house structures and one below the corner post of a house. [78] Burials of the dead under occupied houses was also common in the American Southwest.

---

[78] Butler, Mary. *Three Archaeological Sites in Somerset County Pennsylvania.* Bulletin No. 753. Harrisburg: Pennsylvania Historical Commission 1939, 13.

Modern Americans may be most familiar with the scaffold burials commonly practiced by the Plains Indians into the late 1800's. Writing in 1881 Yarrow, using the commonly applied superior tones of the nineteenth-century white scholar, stated, "These Indians being in all things most superstitious, attach a kind of sacredness to these scaffolds and all the materials used or about the dead. This superstition is in itself sufficient to prevent any of their own people from disturbing the dead, and for one of another nation to in any wise meddle with them is considered an offense not too severely punished by death. The same feeling also prevents them from ever using old scaffolds or any of the wood which has been used about them, even for firewood, though the necessity may be very great, for fear some evil consequences will follow. It is also the custom, though not universally followed, when bodies have been for two years on the scaffolds to take them down and bury them under ground...In case the dead was a man of importance, or if the family could afford it, even though he were not, one or several horses (generally, in the former case, those which the departed thought most of) are shot and placed under the scaffold. The idea in this is that the spirit of the horse will accompany and be of use to his spirit in the "happy hunting grounds," or, as these people express it, 'the spirit land.'" [79]

---

[79] Yarrow, op cit.

Scaffold burials were important to the Sioux as this method of disposal gave the body back to the elements. "It is left exposed to the agents of heaven," stated Black Elk, "the four winds, the rains, the wingeds of the air, each of which—and with the Earth—absorbs a part."[80]

Early 19th century depiction of the Chippewa scaffold burial.

The Chippewa not only used the scaffold to dispose of their dead but also placed the remains in a box which was placed on the scaffold. An 1827 account of such a burial was given by Thomas L. McKenney of the Chippewas of Fond du Lac, Wisconsin:

"One mode of burying the dead among the Chippewas is to place the coffin or box containing their remains on two cross-pieces, nailed or tied with wattap to four poles. The poles are about ten feet high. They plant near these posts

---

[80] Brown, Joseph Epes, ed. *The Sacred Pipe: Black Elk's Account of the Seven Rites of the Oglala Sioux.* Norman: University of Oklahoma Press 1953 & 1989, 14

the wild hop or some other kind of running vine, which spreads over and covers the coffin. I saw one of these on the island, and as I have described it. It was the coffin of a child about four years old. It was near the lodge of the sick girl. I have a sketch of it. I asked the chief why his people disposed of their dead in that way. He answered they did not like to put them out of their sight so soon by putting them under ground. Upon a platform they could see the box that contained their remains, and that was a comfort to them."

Other means of burial included placing the body on the ground and building a pen around it with sticks and logs. This means was utilized by the Sauks, Foxes, and Pottawatomies. Two 19th century illustrations of pen burials are shown below:

In some tribes when someone died in their home the body was removed through a hole cut in the wall and the hole immediately repaired. In this way the ghost, should it return to earth, would be unable to find the doorway and thus kept from haunting it's old abode.

5 Ghost Keeping

As previously discussed, ghost "keeping" is a practice among the Sioux of "keeping" a spirit, or soul, of a loved one (particularly a favorite son) soon after death. The spirit is kept to appease it, to enable it to easily move on to the spirit land. This is an optional thing for the family to do and a ceremony called *Wanagi yuhapi* ("ghost, they keep") is performed. When performed the spirit, or ghost, will be kept for six months to two years. "A ghost is kept," wrote William Powers, "so that by the proper rites it will be assured a return to its origin, and because the lingering ghost will help people to be mindful of death." [81]

This important ritual was outlawed by the government in 1890 following the Wooded Knee massacre. By order of the government, the Sioux were also required to release all of the souls kept on a specific day. (See the Appendix for an account of this rite as observed in 1882.)

The intent of the "Keeping of the Soul" ritual was to purify the soul so that it is "able to return to the 'place' where it was born—*Wakan-Tanka*—and need not wander about the earth as is the case with the souls of bad people; further, the keeping of the soul helps us to remember death and also *Wakan-Tanka,* who is above all dying." [82]

Nineteenth century ethnologist H.C. Yarrow described "Ghost Keeping" in his report to the Bureau of American Ethnology:

"Still another custom, though at the present day by no means generally followed, is still observed to some extent among them. This is called *wanagee yuhapee,* or "keeping the ghost." A little of the hair from the head of the deceased being preserved is bound up in calico and articles of value until the roll is about two feet long and ten inches or more in diameter, when it is placed in a case made of hide handsomely ornamented with various designs in different

---

[81] Powers, William K. *Oglala Religion.* Lincoln: University of Nebraska Press 1977, 93.

[82] Brown, Joseph Epes, ed. *The Sacred Pipe: Black Elk's Account of the Seven Rites of the Oglala Sioux.* Norman: University of Oklahoma Press 1953, 1989, 11.

colored paints. When the family is poor, however, they may substitute for this case blue or scarlet blanket or cloth. The roll is then swung lengthwise between two supports made of sticks, placed thus × in front of a lodge which has been set apart for the purpose. In this lodge are gathered presents of all kinds, which are given out when a sufficient quantity is obtained. It is often a year and sometimes several years before this distribution is made. During all this time the roll containing the hair of the deceased is left undisturbed in front of the lodge. The gifts as they are brought in are piled in the back part of the lodge, and are not to be touched until given out. No one but men and boys are admitted to the lodge unless it be a wife of the deceased, who may go in if necessary very early in the morning. The men sit inside, as they choose, to smoke, eat, and converse. As they smoke they empty the ashes from their pipes in the center of the lodge, and they, too, are left undisturbed until after the distribution. When they eat, a portion is always placed first under the roll outside for the spirit of the deceased. No one is allowed to take this unless a large quantity is so placed, in which case it may be eaten by any persons actually in need of food, even though strangers to the dead. When the proper time comes the friends of the deceased and all to whom presents are to be given are called together to the lodge and the things are given out by the man in charge. Generally this is some near relative of the departed. The roll is now undone and small locks of the hair distributed with the other presents, which ends the ceremony.

"Sometimes this 'keeping the ghost' is done several times, and it is then looked upon as a repetition of the burial or putting away of the dead. During all the time before the distribution of the hair, the lodge, as well as the roll, is looked upon as in a manner sacred, but after that ceremony it becomes common again and may be used for any ordinary purpose. No relative or near friend of the dead wishes to retain anything in his possession that belonged to him while living, or to see, hear, or own anything which will remind him of the departed. Indeed, the leading idea in all their burial customs in the laying away with the dead their most valuable possessions, the giving to others what is left of his and the family property, the refusal to mention his name, &c., is to put out of mind as soon and as effectual as possible the memory of the departed.

"From what has been said, however, it will be seen that they believe each person to have a spirit which continues to live after the death of the body. They have no idea of a future life in the body, but believe that after death their spirits will meet and recognize the spirits of their departed friends in the spirit land. They deem it essential to their happiness here, however, to destroy as far as practicable their recollection of the dead. They frequently speak of death as a sleep, and of the dead as asleep or having gone to sleep at such a time. These customs are gradually losing their hold upon them, and are much less generally and strictly observed than formerly."[83]

As part of the ritual the family gives away all of its personal belongings to the needy members of the tribe in memory of the ghost.

A special tipi is then erected for the ghost to reside in. Prior to this a lock of hair is cut from the deceased and placed in a new cloth or skin and put away for four days. After four days, the bundle is wrapped in a buckskin bag along with a ceremonial pipe. The bundle is now approximately two feet long and six inches wide. To ensure that the tribe knows that the ghost will be kept, the father of the deceased takes the bundle in his arms, as he would an infant, mounts his horse and rides around the camp.

Eventually the bundle is placed in the tipi where the family must carefully care for it. The parents must feed the ghost each day with berry juice and meat. According to Black Elk the meat is sun dried and pounded together with wild cherries and tallow obtained from the bones of buffalo. A selection of this food is kept in a buffalo-hide box specially painted and saved for the day when the soul is set free. The bundle is set outside on nice days and when the camp moves to another location the bundle and all of its associated

---

[83] Yarrow, H.C. "A further contribution to the study of the mortuary customs of the North American Indians," *First Annual Report of the Bureau of Ethnology to the Secretary of the Smithsonian Institution*, Government Printing Office, Washington, 1881, pages 87-204.

belongings is put on a special pack animal, or "ghost horse" and transported to the new location.

On the day prior to the ghost's release a "spirit post" is carved by a holy person. The post represents the deceased and is placed inside the spirit tipi. On the release day a ritual called *wakicagapi* ("they do something for it") is performed with the family, friends and other tribal members participating. The ritual is followed by a feast wherein the ghost is fed for the last time. "Women enter the spirit lodge," Powers relates, "each in turn hugging the spirit post and lamenting. The articles of clothing and other utensils are then given away...The clothing of the family, all its personal belonging, horses, and tipi are given away and the family is left impoverished." [84] Later relatives and friends give new clothing and other necessary items to the family to start their lives anew.

In discussing the ghost keeping ritual, William Powers wrote, "the dead body is wrapped and placed on a burial scaffold or in a tree. The spirit is fed for the last time by placing food in the ground. Here, wrapping is symbolic of darkness, metaphorically a return to one's subterranean origins. The depression in the earth into which food is placed is offset by the accretion of the burial scaffold." [85]

On the day of release the keeper of the soul speaks to the spirit contained in the bundle:

"You, O soul, were with your people but soon you will leave. Today is your day, and it is *waken.* Today your Father, *Wakan-Tanka*, is bending down to see you; all your people have arrived to be with you. All your relatives love you, and have taken good care of you...Behold! This is the sacred day!" [86]

The custom of "feeding the dead" was fairly common. This practice was not strictly a form of "ghost keeping" however. The Yokaia, "Ukiah" according to the settlers, had a custom to "feed the spirits of the dead" over a years period of time. According to Stephen Powers, an ethnologist for the Department of Interior in the late 19th century, the Yokaia went "daily to places which they (the dead) were accustomed to frequent while living, where they sprinkle pinole upon the ground. A Yokaia mother who has lost her babe goes every day for a year to some place her little one played while

---

[84] Ibid., 95.

[85] Powers, William K., op cit., 182.

[86] Brown, op cit., 22.

alive, or the spot where its body was burned, and milks her breast into the air." [87]

The Chumash also fed the dead. According to Chumash tradition people would place food on the graves of the recently buried over a five-day period. "They would cook meals early," according to Blackburn, "and at about four-o'clock in the afternoon they would sit down to mourn and to scatter food. They scattered it with their hands, they scattered it to the four winds." [88]

In the Oglala Sioux tradition, after death an individual's close relative may chose to undertake the duties of a mourner. These duties last for one year. As part of the functions of mourning, the individual must talk to and ritually feed the spirit. A place-setting is reserved at the table with meat and water provided. When the meal is over the water is poured on the ground and the meat is burned or buried. This undertaking is dangerous for the relative however, as the daily feeding cannot be ignored or forgotten lest the spirit will become angry and possibly harmful. After the last meal is provided to the spirit the spirit then journeys on to its place in the afterworld in the Milky Way.

---

[87] Powers, Stephen. *Tribes of California.* Berkeley: University of California Press 1976, 166-167.

[88] Blackburn, Thomas C. *December's Child: A Book of Chumash Oral Narratives.* Berkeley: University of California Press 1975, 97.

19th century painting of Dakota mourners offering food to the dead.

6 Ghosts in the Dream World

A ccording to Jackson Lincoln, "The dream was the reality experience of the soul or shadow while the body slept. Belief in ghosts, apparitions, specters and spirits also arose from the same course. In like manner, there grew up the belief in the continued, permanent or temporary, existence of the soul after death, since evidence of their dreams showed it alive and confronting them. Moreover, in their dreams many primitives visited the abode of the dead and returned to tell about it." [89]

Dreams are the "information highways" for ghosts and spirits. They impart warnings, instruct, communicate desires and inflict harm through dreams. Many times these sleep-time visitations are the only form of visitation that the living may receive. And many of these dreams are believed to be dangerous. According to ethnographer Morris Opler who studied the Apache in depth, "The most terrifying dream of all is that in which one accepts food from a deceased relative, for such acceptance...is a sign of immanent death." [90]

Similar beliefs were held by the Yuman tribes along the Gila River. An informant who was a member of the Haldhidhoma tribe stated, "A person dreams he is in the land of the dead. If he eats anything given to him there, he gets sick. A person might dream of this repeatedly, join in the games there, and thinking it fun, dream of it every night. Such a person would faint," lose his soul and die. [91]

Other tribes believe that dreams, specifically of dead relatives and friends, are imparting information to help the living. Dreams are often viewed as a form of mediation between the living and the dead. "These spirits," according to Mark St. Pierre, "have made a happy journey to the other side and either have returned by their

---

[89] Lincoln, Jackson Steward. *The Dream in Native American and Other Primitive Cultures.* Mineola: Dover Publications, Inc. 2003, 44.

[90] Opler, Morris Edward. *An Apache Life-Way.* Chicago: The University of Chicago Press 1941, 234.

[91] Spier, Leslie. *Yuman Tribes of the Gila River.* New York: Dover Publications, Inc. 1978, 297.

own will or were sent by the Great Spirit." [92] Some Plains tribes believe that ghosts should not be feared but respected and treated as they were in life.

Dreams are direct communications with the spirit world and while they may be both welcomed and feared, they can never be ignored. Among the Paiute "If a person dreams of a ghost and if the ghost touches him, or if he dreams about someone who is dead, the ghost is said to take away his thought." [93] When this happens, illness will soon follow for "take away his thought" is the same as taking away the breath, resulting in "ghost sickness."

Dreams are powerful. They import information from the Otherworld. They allow the spirit to travel to other places and times. Dreams allow the soul to visit the dead in the afterworld and for the dead to visit the living. The Iroquois interpret dreams as the wishes of the soul.

Dreams as a communication means between the living and the dead was commonly accepted. "...communication through dreams and visions between the human beings living in 'our land' and the deceased living in the 'other land', wrote Jean-Guy Goulet, "is possible and normal" to the Canadian Dene Tha Indians. [94] The dreams we all experience are directly due to the wandering soul's travels according to many Native people.

The dual aspect of the soul is an important aspect of the dream. Obviously, the soul leaves the body at death but is also capable of wandering in the dream state. This is a dangerous time for the soul as it may be "kidnapped" by spirits or ghosts in which case the body will eventually die. Mauzé noted, "It's outings can be dangerous, because it can be attracted by ghosts to the land of the dead." [95]

---

[92] St. Pierre, Mark and Tilda Long Soldier. *Walking in the Sacred Manner.* New York: Touchstone Books/Simon & Schuster 1995, 122.

[93] Whiting, Beatrice Blyth. *Paiute Sorcery.* New York: The Viking Fund Publications in Anthropology Number Fifteen 1950, 35.

[94] Goulet, Jean-Guy A. "Reincarnation as a Fact of Life among Contemporary Dene Tha" in *Amerindian Rebirth.* Toronto: University of Toronto Press 1994, 159.

[95] Mauzé, Marie. "The Concept of the Person and Reincarnation among the Kwakiutl Indians," in *Amerindian Rebirth.* Toronto: University of Toronto Press 1994, 180.

"The fear of death," wrote Jackson Lincoln of the Kwakiutl, "and murderous cannibalistic wishes are most evident in dreams, myths and ceremonies in which even dead bodies are eaten. Out of 63 individual dreams recorded 28 are of the dead, and many of these of the dead father, grandfather or relatives and dead lovers." [96] To the Kwakiutl, nightmares indicated the death of a near relative and dreams of cohabitating with a dead woman signified bad luck.

Dreams of death are not necessarily a foretelling of the demise of the dreamer but may indicate that he/she was in the afterworld with the spirits of the dead. However, the Navajo believed that a dream wherein the dead beckon to the dreamer or the dreamer shakes hands with a dead spirit does mean that death is imminent.

Dreams are a reflection of cultural teachings. They may indicate illness, they may impart knowledge that has been hidden away in the recesses of the mind, they may allow the dreamer to understand events in his life and how to deal with them. Ghostly visits in dreams may actually indicate that a spiritual exchange has taken place between the dead and the living as part of a paranormal experience—and thus proof of the existence of spirits and the spirit world. Many dreams of Native Americans were believed to indicate that an individual was to undertake a course of learning to be a healer and/or shaman. The teacher? The spirits and souls of those who appear in these important dreams.

---

[96] Lincoln, op cit., 150.

7 The Spirit Land

Most every culture believes in the existence of the soul after death. Usually the afterworld was a duplicate of the earthly existence of the deceased although much more pleasant with abundant game, beautiful mountains, rivers and forests. Usually the soul also must meet certain tests to transition from the physical world to the land of the dead.

Many of these tests call for the spirit to cross vast chasms with narrow passageways or traverse over massive waterfalls while monstrous creatures attempt to pull the soul into oblivion.

"Ghosts live under the earth," write anthropologist Marie Mauzé, "the underworld being 'the habitat of people after they have left their humanness.' Their villages are similar to those of human beings. But night and day are inverted. The underworld or 'lowest world' is conceived as one of reversal." [97]Mauzé was writing about the Kwakiutl on the Pacific Northwest but similar concepts were held by other Native peoples as well.

The afterworld of the Lakota Sioux is in the northern sky. Here the departed live on in peace and plenty free of illness and sorrow. They spent their eternity playing games, singing, dancing and hunting as they wished. It is said that "agreeable women and fine horses" [98] are also there to make the afterworld an even finer experience.

In Lakota myth, the spirits of cowards or mean spirited people are met by the Spirit of the North on a narrow trail on the path to the Otherworld. The Spirit of the North trips the soul so that it falls into the waters, which separate the land of the living and the land of the dead, the Spirit of Waters is allowed to do as it will with the fallen soul. [99] Another Lakota tradition says that after death the soul "must cross a river on a very narrow tree. If he is afraid to cross the river,

---

[97] Mauzé, Marie. "The Concept of the Person and Reincarnation among the Kwakiutl Indians" in *Amerindian Rebirth: Reincarnation Belief Among North American Indians and Inuit.* Toronto: University of Toronto Press 1990, 181.

[98] Walker, James R. *Lakota: Belief and Ritual.* Lincoln: University of Nebraska Press 1991, 123

[99] Ibid.

he returns to the world and wanders about forever. If he crosses the river, he goes to the spirit world." [100]

The theme of the soul crossing over an abyss by walking over a narrow ledge is a widespread one. In every case, the soul is threatened with monsters, guardians of the otherworld and other varied distractions, which attempt to pull the soul into swirling waters or into deep crevasses so that it is not able to reach the underworld where eternal life is waiting.

Native Americans believed in an existence after death, the quality of which depended on how an individual lived and died. The Nahuatl believed that all persons continued to live eternally and that the soul was not affected by the personal behavior of the individual prior to death. The Aztecs, on the other hand, believed in the consequences of acts that were outside those normally accepted. While the Nahuatl believed in a "heaven" where the soul continued to live much as it had on earth, they also believed in the concept of multiple heavens of lesser degrees—somewhat similar to the Christian concept of purgatory.

The Luiseño Indians in Southern California, according to Moriarty, "recognize that there was something within the body that did not die with the flesh." [101]

The Luiseño believed that when one died the soul went to a heavenly place ruled by Chinigchinix, the god. The Luiseño conceived of this heaven as a place similar to the terrestrial world that they lived in but with a sense that sadness and work were no longer evident. Another belief was that the soul would travel to heaven and become a new star in the night sky. In those cases where an individual died away from their traditional lands it was felt that Chinigchinix would decide if the soul was worthy to live on in heaven or not.

The Gabrielino, a neighboring tribe to the Luiséno, believed that the hearts of fully initiated tribal members took their places as stars in the heavens. The other, more ordinary members, "went to an underworld where they made merry with dancing and feasting." [102]

---

[100] Ibid., 71.

[101] Moriarty, James Robert. *Chinigchinix: An Indigenous California Indian Religion.* Los Angeles: Southwest Museum 1969, 50.

[102] Johnston, Bernice Eastman. *California's Gabrielino Indians.* Los Angeles: Southwest Museum 1962, 53.

Like other groups the Garbrielino believed that the Milky Way was the home of the spirit—at least for those initiated members.

Another California tribe, the Pomo, believe that the afterworld is in the heavens as well. To get there after death the Pomo believe that "they will ascend by a ladder. The souls of the wicked will fall off the ladder in the ascent and descend into negative and nondescript limbo, where they will be neither happy nor tormented, but rove vacantly and idly forevermore." [103] The truly evil, however, are transformed into the grizzly bear or the rattlesnake which must crawl over the burning sand or be forever hungry.

The Coast Miwok believed that the dead leapt into the sea at Point Reyes and followed a string through the surf to the west and the setting sun where they resided with Coyote in the afterlife. In many native traditions Coyote plays a major role as both trickster and a cultural hero who created the earth, caused death, taught the people about fire and generally brought knowledge to humankind.

The Hupa Indians residing in the far northwestern corner of California believed in a "damp, dark underworld" with only the spirits of shamans and singers who participated in major ceremonies allowed to journey on to a more pleasant afterworld in the sky. Other California tribes as well, such as the neighboring Karok, believed that the afterworld was established along class lines. The Karok did believe that the spirits of all dead journeyed to an afterlife in the sky, however, "an especially happy place was reserved for rich people and ceremonial leaders." [104]

The Karok soul must chose between two paths after death. One was a path of roses which leads to the "Happy Western Land beyond the great water" and the other a path of thorns and briers which leads to a dark land of evil. [105]

Another Northern California tribe, the Mattoal, believe that the afterworld lays southward in the Great Ocean. The souls of the bad did not journey on to the afterworld but transformed into the grizzly bear which was representative of sin.

---

[103] Powers, Stephen. *Tribes of California.* Berkeley: University of California Press 1976,161.

[104] Bright, William. "Karok" in *Handbook of North American Indians: Vol. 8- California.* Washington: Smithsonian Institution 1978,186.

[105] Powers, Stephen. *Tribes of California* Berkeley: University of California Press 1976, 34.

The Mandan Indians of the plains believed that the soul returned to the subterranean world that was, according to mythology, the place of origin for the Mandan people.

The Assinniboin and Athapascan tribes believed that upon death the soul migrated toward the south where the climate was warm and the game abundant. The Assinniboin concept of hell was, naturally, the reverse of this. Hell was a land of perpetual ice and snow and a lack of everything desirable.

The Creeks simply believed that the souls of the good went to an afterlife in the sky while those of evil people "went west."

Hidatsa concepts of the afterlife were quite developed and were similar to the concepts of the ancient Greeks. Washington Matthews, a 19th century ethnologist, wrote in an 1877 study:

"When a Hidatsa dies his shade (soul) lingers four nights around the camp or village in which he died, and then goes to the lodge of his departed kindred in the village of the dead. When he arrives there he is rewarded for his valor, self denial, and ambition on earth by receiving the same regard in the one place as in the other; for there, as here, the brave man is honored and the coward despised."[106]

Individuals who committed suicide also went to this afterworld but had to remain separated from the others—in a form of purgatory.

The Hidatsa concept of heaven is similar to the concepts of other religions—life continues although somewhat altered. The souls of humans hunted and fed off the "shades" or souls of animals that had died on earth. A lifestyle exactly the same as the earthly one was maintained. This new world of the afterlife appeared little different except that the four seasons were reversed in their order.

In Virginia, the Sapona Indians believed in a supreme god and believed that upon death all souls were taken under guard to the "great road" where the good and evil souls traveled together until they reached a fork in the road. One lane of the road was level and

---

[106] Matthews, Washington. *Ethnological and Philol. Of Hidatsa Indians.* Washington: U.S. Geological and Geographical Survey, Misc. Publications #7, 1877, 49.

clean, the other strewn with rocks, and mountainous. The good and bad souls eventually were separated by strikes of lightning. [107]

According to legend, the level road, the path on the right taken by the good souls lead to a "charming warm country" where time did not exist and the weather perpetually like May. The souls, upon reaching this land, lived much as they had on the earth with one exception: everything that was attempted was successfully accomplished. The animals were plentiful and fat. At the entryway to this land of plenty sat an old man who, like St. Peter, determined if the soul was worthy to enter.

The left path, covered with debris, lead to a land of perpetual hunger. A "bitter kind of potato" was the only source of food, which gave the soul-body great ulcers. The land was covered with another miserable thing—an eternal blanket of snow. According to Sapona legend, the women who resided in this hell were all ugly and attacked the men constantly with their unbridled passions. To make things worse they could only communicate in shrill tones. The ruler of this afterworld was an ancient, ugly woman with serpent-like hair. It was her only duty to determine the various degrees and period of torture with the type and amount of torture given out depending on the amount of sins accumulated by the soul. If, after the period of torture was completed, the soul had repented of its crimes it was allowed to travel on to "the regions of bliss."

Like the Sapona, the Natchez also had a very defined concept of the afterlife. They believed so strongly in a heaven with abundant feasting, dancing women and pleasure that the men willingly went to their deaths in battle so that they would enter this afterworld sooner. The Natchez also believed in a hell in which the soul was left naked, exposed to mosquitoes, the world covered in water, and food limited to spoiled fish.

The Pawnee's belief system of an afterlife was included in their cosmological views. The Pawnee believed that some souls traveled to the heavens to become stars while other souls belong to those who died of illness or cowardice forever traveled the Milky Way, also referred to as the "ghost road" from end to end. Of course, the

---

[107] Byrd, William. *History of the Dividing Line*, Vol. 1, 1792 (reprinted 1866), 106-108.

chiefs, shamans and priests all ascended to a distant heavenly village.

"When at last it shakes free of its corporal abode," wrote Hoebel, "the Cheyenne soul wafts free and light up the Hanging Road to dwell thereafter in benign proximity to the Great Wise one and the lonng-lost loved ones. Only the souls of those who have committed suicide are barred from this peace." [108] Where these souls wind up is not revealed however although the Cheyenne do not have a Hell.

Existence on the Hanging Road, a world suspended between the heavens and the earth, is just as it was for the Cheyenne while they were living. "All the Cheyennes of the past live in heaven, just as they did on earth—and have a good time of it," states anthropologist Hoebel. [109]

The Hopi Indians of the American Southwest believed in the immortality of the soul and that an afterlife was lived in a parallel world to that experienced on the earth during their lives. The soul was believed to live, work and play in the same manner as the individual had on earth. However, the soul also was thought to have the ability to float in the clouds and to bring rain to the physical world.

According to Hattie Lockett, writing in 1933 about the Hopi, "If the adult spirit has led a good life, it goes to the abode where the ancestral spirits feast and hold ceremonies as on earth, but if evil it must be tried by fire and, if too bad for purification, it is destroyed."[110]

Contrary to the Hopi, the Navajo have an extreme fear and avoidance of anything having to do with death. The afterworld is, according to Kluckhohn, "a shadowy and uninviting thing." [111] The Navajo believe that the afterworld is just like the physical world of the living but located in the north just below the earth's surface. The

---

[108] Hoebel, E. Adamson. *The Cheyennes: Indians of the Great Plains.* New York: Holt, Rinehart and Winston, Case Studies in Cultural Anthropology 1960, 87.

[109] Ibid., 86.

[110] Lockett, Hattie Greene. "The Unwritten Literature of the Hopi," *Social Science Bulletin Number 2, Vol. IV, Number 4,* May 15, 1933. Tucson: University of Arizona

[111] Kluckhohn, Clyde and Dorothea Leighton. *The Navaho.* Garden City: Anchor Books 1962, 184.

spirit must travel down a trail until they reach a sandpile at the bottom. Here the spirits deceased relatives, who look just as they did while living, guide the soul to the afterworld which takes a four day journey. The Navajo underworld is neither one of pleasure and beauty or of pain but is only dreary.

Kluckhohn's statement about the Navajo afterworld, however, is contradictory with research by other anthropologists. While the Navajo feared ghosts, thereby believing in an existence after death, Reichard noted that the idea of personal immortality as a personality was not widely held. "Rather," she stated, "the individual becomes universal; at death the person is left behind with the body." [112] As a matter of clarification Reichard adds "Indifference about the afterlife doubtless reflects the ethical system, which holds that man suffers here on earth, if at all, but need not expect punishment after death; the individual spirit may be lost in the cosmos." [113]

In Apache tradition "the ghost of the departed makes its way or is led by other ghostly kin to the underworld, 'a beautiful place beneath the ground, where a nice stream of water flows between banks that are lined with cottonwood trees, and everything is green.'" [114]

The way to this beautiful world was through an opening in the ground "cut out like a window." This opening is hidden by tall grass and the departed soul must be led to it so that it isn't missed. Once inside the opening, however, it is almost impossible to return.

An individual who had a "near death experience" described this afterworld:

"The same ways we have here are carried on down there too. Those people dance, eat, and sleep. A person down there can actually feel another in the flesh. The people remain the same age as they were when they died. I saw people as they were when they went. That is the way it is always seen. There is no sickness, death, pain, or sorrow there...The same places, the same sacred

---

[112] Reichard, Gladys A. *Navaho Religion: A Study of Symbolism.* Princeton: Princeton University Press 1950, 33.

[113] Ibid., 41.

[114] Opler, Morris Edward. *An Apache Life-Way.* Chicago: The University of Chicago Press 1941, 477.

mountains, the same ceremonies exist there as here. It is just as though everything is transferred to a different country." [115]

The spirit land, according to the Maricopa, was a duplicate of the physical world of the living, except day and night and the seasons were reversed. "The dead were constantly at dances and games," wrote Spier, "so many of them together that there were crowds at the games. They went to war. They were always enjoying themselves, with plenty to eat." [116]

In the Maricopa afterworld, as in so many others, the old became young and "old things new." However, babies matured to age fifteen or so. The dead who inhabit this afterworld mate and have children. "Living" in the land of the dead was not eternal however. The inhabitants eventually get old and die again—in fact they have three lives and die three times. At the fourth death the soul becomes "nothing more than a bit of charcoal lying in the desert." [117] The only complaint voiced by the Maricopa dead is how rapidly they could travel:

"When a living person wanted to go somewhere, he had the pleasure of anticipation and fulfillment: he set a day and on that day went off camping enroute for however long it might take him. 'But with us,' the dead complain, 'when we want to go anywhere, we are there before we know. We do not like that.'"[118]

The Indians in Northern California living in the Lassen volcano area believed that the dead lived on much as they had in life—using sweat houses, hunting, sleeping and carrying on as they always had. The major difference is that sickness no longer exists. No clear picture of their ancient beliefs can be obtained however since after the white settlers arrived the Native traditions became heavily influenced with Christian dogma. These people believed that after death the soul would go south where it was 'evaluated" and, after passing the evaluation, it would travel to a distant place in the west by way of the Milky Way. [119]

---

[115] Ibid., 478.

[116] Spier, Lesli. *Yuman Tribes of the Gila River*. New York: Dover Publications, Inc. 1978, 298.

[117] Ibid.

[118] Ibid.

[119] Schulz, Paul E. *Indians of Lassen*. Mineral: Loomis Museum Association 1954, 152.

Many Native American stories of the afterlife speak of the dead hunting as they had in life. What exactly did they hunt? According to Father Paul Le Jeune, who wrote of the Montagnais Indians in 1634, "They hunt for the souls of beavers, porcupines, moose, and other animals, using the soul of the snowshoes to walk upon the soul of the snow, which is in yonder country; in short, they make use of the souls of all things, as we here use the things themselves."[120]

The Chumash Indians of California's Santa Barbara coastal area believed that the soul is eternal and reincarnation a normal part of the cycle. However, there are differences in the final disposition of the spirit. "The dead go west and are born again in this world," writes anthropologist Thomas Blackburn. "It is all a circle, an eddy within the abyss." [121] After death, unless cremated, the spirit remains in the area where they lived for five days. Those who were cremated immediately go to the west and do not remain for the five day period to pass. The souls of those drowned, however, always remained in the sea, never reaching land and never being reborn. Likewise souls of infants never reached the afterworld of the adults. Most souls, who did not drown or were infants at death, traveled west where they remained for twelve years. At the end of the twelve years the soul would be reborn. During this time, the soul was free to travel the world although they inhabited another sphere, far in the west.

The Chumash believed that the dead found their way to the afterworld through a sacred pool at Point Humqaq. Point Humqaq was so holy that all Chumash avoided it except for periodic pilgrimages to leave offerings at the shrine. Point Humqaq was viewed as a "portal" used by the souls of the Chumash to reach heaven where they awaited their turn at reincarnation. Humqaq Pool, located nearby, is a basin in which fresh water continuously drips and where the Chumash spirit "bathes and paints itself" while waiting to ascend to heaven. [122] Today these sacred sites are

---

[120] Ashton, John and Tom Whyte. *The Quest for Paradise.* New York: HarperSanFrancisco 2001, 148.

[121] Blackburn, Thomas G. *December's Child: A Book of Chumash Oral Narratives.* Berkeley: University of California Press 1975, 97.

[122] Anderson, John. *Kuta Teachings: Reincarnation Theology of the Chumash Indians of California.* Kootenai: American Designs Publishing 1998, 49

inaccessible being located on private property on two massive ranches, the Hollister Ranch and the 8700 acre Cojo Ranch.

The Chumash myth *The Soul's Journey to Šimilaqša* tells of the soul's journey from the grave to Point Conception where the sacred pool is located. The story says that "there in the stone can be seen the footprints of women and children. There the spirit of the dead bathes and paints itself. Then it sees a light to the westward and goes toward it through the air, and thus reaches the land of Šimilaqša ('land of the dead across the sea')." [123]

The souls of the Chumash dead must cross a river or pool that separates the world of the living from the world of the dead, as they did at the River Styx and other boundaries throughout the legends of many other cultures. A slender pole is dropped across the water on which the soul must walk to the other side. To complicate the issue two water monsters attempt to dislodge each soul as it crosses the pole, if they fall they are doomed to be transformed into a being with both human and frog-like attributes, forced to live in the waters for eternity. The myth goes on to say that the souls of murderers and other evil people are turned to stone and do not cross the river but must watch as the other souls are allowed to cross throughout time.

Chumash rock art depicting supernatural figures, including the centipede that represents death. (Painted Cave, Santa Barbara, California, photo by Gary R. Varner)

---

[123] Blackburn, op cit. 98.

Close up of two ghost figures at Painted Cave. Supposedly, these figures represent souls that are lost in the supernatural world. (Photo by Gary R. Varner)

Far to the north, the Netsilik Eskimo believed that there are three afterworlds. The first is called "the village," or *Agneriartarfik*. Located in the sky, this afterworld provides an abundance of game with caribou in huge herds. If, however, the spirit tires of hunting and eating caribou "the moon spirit helps them down to the sea where they can kill seals." [124] This afterworld is beautiful with good weather and the residents "continuously happy." The dead play at games and everything is supposedly happiness and fun. This afterworld is reserved for hunters who have died violently and for women who have undergone the pains of receiving large and beautiful tattoos. The dead remain at their age when they died.

The second afterworld is located in the underworld, deep beneath the tundra. Called *Aglermiut*, the dead here experience the same benefits that the dead in *Agneriartarfik* receive. Salmon fishing and caribou hunting are excellent and the dead live on in happiness and abundance. The main difference between this afterworld and the physical world is that the seasons are reversed. *Aglermiut* is populated with hunters and tattooed women as *Agneriartarfik* is.

---

[124] Balikci, Asen. *The Netsilik Eskimo*. Garden City: The Natural History Press 1970, 214.

The third afterworld, called *Noqumiut*, is also located underground and just below the earth's crust. This world is reserved for the lazy hunter and women who would not undergo the pain of receiving tattoos. The residents here huddle together with hanging heads and closed eyes. They are perpetually hungry and apathetic with the only food the butterfly, which can only be caught if it flies too close to the head of a dead man or woman.

As in most cultures, those individuals who break societal rules or who do not contribute to the wellbeing of the whole are punished. In Netsilik society, the lazy and idle received the most severe punishment after death.

The Tillamook Indians on the Oregon Coast believed that after death the soul had to travel a long distance to reach the world of the dead. After two days of walking a river was reached where the soul had to wait for ten days. After ten days, a canoe crossed the river to get the soul and take it to the other side. On the other side, all the other souls had gathered in a large house to greet the individual. Dancing and feasting soon commenced. This land is said to be beautiful with colorful birds and plentiful game and fish to take. The best thing is that the old are young once more. The Tillamook also believed that the vast schools of salmon were also composed of the spirits of dead ancestors who returned to Tillamook Bay each year to provide food to those still living. The spirits reincarnated as salmon hope to be captured by their descendents.[125]

The Sanpoil Indians of Washington State believed that the soul had two alternatives after death, "it could go at once to the land of the dead at the end of the Milky Way in the sky; or it could be transformed into a ghost and remain on earth. If it went to the land of the dead, it never returned to earth or communicated with men on earth. It gave up all individual activity and assumed a nirvana-like status...Everyone hoped his soul would attain the limbo of the land of the dead and not remain on earth as a ghost in a condition of perpetual torment."[126]

Sanpoil ghosts appeared as shadowy figures clothed in opaque garb. Most appeared without heads or other parts of the body and

---

[125] Sauter, John and Bruce Johnson. *Tillamook Indians of the Oregon Coast.* Portland: Binfords & Mort, Publishers 1974, 40.

[126] Driver, Harold E. *Indians of North America, 2nd edition.* Chicago: University of Chicago Press 1969, 419.

could be seen both during the day and at night but never to more than one person at a time.

New England tribes had similar beliefs in the afterworld as other tribes across North America. The Narragansetts, who occupied much of Rhode Island, believed that the soul consisted of two parts. One was believed to exist while the body slept and the other which was a reflection of the body. After death one of them continued to an afterlife similar to the physical existence during the time the individual lived. This afterlife existed for the souls of "great and good men and women" who lived on in the house of the creator, Cautántowwit. The souls of murderers, thieves and liars were sentenced to an existence of continuous wandering and restlessness.

The Algonquians of Virginia had two philosophies regarding an afterlife. The upper class believed that only chiefs and shamans could expect a life after death. However, the majority of Algonquian believed in reincarnation and survival after death.

The Algonquians of North Carolina also believed in an afterlife structured according to the individual's moral conduct. Those with evil souls were believed to go to a pit of fire in the west while reincarnation was commonly viewed as an outcome for most.

The Huron believed that after death and after the Feast of the Dead had been performed, souls "would assemble covered in their robes and grave goods and depart on a path along the Milky Way." [127] The souls of the very young or the elderly remained in a special village and used the corn fields abandoned by those still living. These earth-bound souls were occasionally noticed but were not feared or considered a threat. In fact, efforts were made by the villagers to keep these souls supplied in provisions.

Those who had been killed in battle or who committed suicide were feared by both the living and those who died peacefully and went to their own villages of the dead. Along the way to the afterworld, souls were faced with obstacles which must be passed. According to Heidenreich, "the souls had to go past the rock *ecaregniondi* in the Petun country. Near this rock lived *oscotarach* 'head-piercer' who drew out their brains and placed them in

---

[127] Heidenreich, Conrad E. "Huron" in *Handbook of North American Indians, Vol. 15: Northeast.* Washington: Smithsonian Institution 1978, 375.

pumpkins. Next, the souls had to pass over a log that lay across a raging river[128] guarded by a fierce dog. Many who were frightened by the dog fell off the log and drowned. After many months, the souls would finally get to the village of the dead, which was very much like that of the living. There they would continue as they had in life, their occupations and status unchanged." [129] These obstacles were only illusions, however, illusions to deceive the souls so that they would not attempt to cross back into the land of the living as ghosts.

Similar heavenly obstacles existed for the [130] Yurok, a Native people of California. According to Powers, "After a death they keep a fire burning certain nights in the vicinity of the grave. They hold and believe, at least the 'Big Indians' do, that the spirits of the departed are compelled to cross an extremely attenuated greased pole, which bridges over the chasm of the 'Debatable Land,' and that they require the fire to light them on their darksome journey. A righteous soul traverses the pole quicker than a wicked one; hence they regulate the number of nights for burning a light according to the character for goodness or the opposite which the deceased possessed in this world."

"The Chippewas," wrote ethnographer H.C. Yarrow, "believe that there is in man an essence entirely distinct from the body; they call it *Ochechag*, and appear to supply to it the qualities which we refer to the soul. They believe that it quits the body it the time of death, and repairs to what they term *Chekechekchekawe*; this region is supposed to be situated to the south, and on the shores of the great ocean. Previous to arriving there they meet with a stream which they are obliged to cross upon a large snake that answers the purpose of a bridge; those who die from drowning never succeed in crossing the stream; they are thrown into it and remain there forever. Some souls come to the edge of the stream, but are prevented from passing by the snake, which threatens to devour them; these are the souls of the persons in a lethargy or trance. Being refused a passage these souls return to their bodies and reanimate them. They believe that animals have souls, and even

---

[128] A common theme in cultural beliefs around the world.

[129] Heidenreich, op cit.

[130] Powers, Stephen. *The Tribes of California*. Berkeley: University of California Press 1976, 58.

that inorganic substances, such as kettles, &c., have in them a similar essence.

"In this land of souls all are treated according to their merits. Those who have been good men are free from pain; they have no duties to perform, their time is spent in dancing and singing, and they feed upon mushrooms, which are very abundant. The souls of bad men are haunted by the phantom of the persons or things that they have injured; thus, if a man has destroyed much property the phantoms of the wrecks of this property obstruct his passage wherever he goes; if he has been cruel to his dogs or horses they also torment him after death. The ghosts of those whom during his lifetime he wronged are there permitted to avenge their injuries. They think that when a soul has crossed the stream it cannot return to its body, yet they believe in apparitions, and entertain the opinion that the spirits of the departed will frequently revisit the abodes of their friends in order to invite them to the other world, and to forewarn them of their approaching dissolution."[131]

The Aztec and Maya, who lived life so close to death, believed in an afterworld of thirteen layers above the earth and nine below. The underworld was a place of fear, dread and darkness. The thirteen layers of heaven above the earth were for a select few who died in battle, in childbirth or even by suicide. Those who died in battle would enter the paradise world of Tonatiuhichán where they would join the sun and take the form of a butterfly or hummingbird. Those who died in water or in storms entered Tlalocán which was a paradise ruled by the rain god Tláloc. Fruit and delicacies were abundant in Tlalocán along with life-giving rain and waterfalls. Those who resided in this paradise could do so in their leisure for work was no longer necessary.

The twelfth and thirteenth layers of heaven were occupied by the Lord of Duality, Ometeotl along with babies who had died before their time and those who died in their sleep inexplicably. These souls would obtain a new life in a new world to be created after the

---

[131] Yarrow, H.C. "A further contribution to the study of the mortuary customs of the North American Indians," *First Annual Report of the Bureau of Ethnology to the Secretary of the Smithsonian Institution*, Government Printing Office, Washington, 1881, pages 87-204.

cataclysm that is to end the fifth sun in the form of a massive earthquake.

One of the Aztec gods was Tlaltecuhtli, a female goddess with a male name meaning "earth lord." Tlaltecuhtli was so feared that sculptures of her almost always found placed face down. She constantly demands appeasement and can only be satisfied with eating the hearts of men or fruit sprinkled with human blood. She was depicted as a woman with huge claws and a stream of blood flowing into her mouth as she squats to give birth, Tlaltecuhtli was believed to devour the dead and then give them new life. While exceedingly fearsome, she was often called upon by midwives to aid in the delivery of children, much as Lilith was in middle eastern cultures.

The Maya believed in an afterworld shaded by the World Tree where the dead spent their time drinking chocolate. The vast majority of the Maya, however, would not enter paradise but rather the underworld of Xibalba, "Realm of Fright," where hellish creatures tormented them unceasingly.

Acording to mythologist John Bierhorst, the Yucatec believed in seven sky levels of the afterworld and say "there is a hole in the center of each of the layers. A ceiba tree, growing at the center of the earth, extends upward through the holes, and it is by climbing this tree that the souls of the dead progress from level to level, eventually reaching the uppermost heaven, where the God of Christianity lives." [132] Like many indigenous people dominated by Christian missionaries a mixture of Native and Christian mythology become accepted, both residing side by side.

Ethnographers have found that in many instances, Christianity dominates the outward appearance of a culture but the older indigenous beliefs and traditions continue unabated. Canadian ethnographer and zoologist Jaques Rousseau stated that Christianity is "a thin veneer covering deep-lying native beliefs." However, the long-term observance of such dual systems eventually creates a single belief system, which incorporates parts of both.

---

[132] Bierhorst, John. *The Mythology of Mexico and Central America.* New York: William Morrow and Company, Inc. 1990, 154.

8 Reincarnation

Many cultures around the world believe, or have believed, in reincarnation—the return of the soul to the world to be reborn. What is the basis for beliefs in reincarnation? According to Antonia Mills, a belief in reincarnation "fits into the basic shamanic belief that typifies hunting and gathering peoples wherever and whenever they are found and...it was probably part of the most ancient human culture."[133] Belief in reincarnation is still prevalent in many parts of the world today, however—and not just in hunter/gatherer societies. In some Native American cultures this belief was modified in that only certain people were believed to be reborn—normally the disabled or deformed who had not been able to live a normal life previously. The Yuman tribes not only believed that the deformed would be reborn but also twins. "They were believed to come from a village of their own, an adjunct of the village of the dead lying to the northwest," wrote Spier. "Some of the deformed there were without arms, others without noses or mouths; some had an eye in the middle of the forehead." [134] Reportedly, twins and the deformed were born on earth as "visitors." These individuals, after death, did not journey on to the land of the dead but returned to their village until they were reborn yet again.

Some Canadian Indians believed that both animals and humans are reincarnated. "The physical features of a newborn child are always referred to those of some dead forebear," noted Werner Müller, "every child is thus a reincarnation." [135]

Generally speaking, the Plains Indians did not have a definite idea of a final afterworld. That is because they believed that reincarnation occurs to allow a soul to be "finished." According to St. Pierre "If the soul does not become complete, dies too soon, or fails successfully to traverse a part of the path of life, then it will be

---

[133] Mills, Antonia. "Reincarnation Belief among North American Indians and Inuit: Context, Distribution, and Variation" in *Amerindian Rebirth: Reincarnation Belief Among North American Indians and Inuit.* Toronto: University of Toronto Press 1994, 18.

[134] Spier, Leslie. *Yuman Tribes of the Gila River.* New York: Dover Publications, Inc. 1978, 299.

[135] Krickeberg, Walter et al., *Pre-Columbian American Religions.* New York: Holt, Rinehart and Winston 1968, 161.

sent back to live on this earth again until it completes the journey 'in a good way.'" [136]

Few in-depth studies have been conducted by anthropologists concerning Native American beliefs in reincarnation. One tribal study by Antonia Mills is that of the Gitxsan on the British Columbia coast. According to Mills, the Gitxsan believe that one soul can be reincarnated simultaneously as multiple people. One such individual reportedly has been reincarnated in seven different bodies since 1987. According to the Gitxsan all of these incarnations "have been within the bodies of her own descendants." [137]

As discussed in the previous chapter, New England tribes, especially the Algonquian, believed that reincarnation was one form of afterlife that was generally available. Like the Narragansetts, the Huron also believed that the individual was composed of at least two souls and possibly as many as five. One stayed near the corpse until a ceremony called the Feast of the Dead was performed. The feast resulted in the soul being set free to be reborn. The other soul went on its own way to a Village of the Dead where life continued much as it had prior to the individual's death. Children younger than one month of age were buried along a well-used pathway so that their soul could reenter the womb of a woman who passed by to be reborn. According to anthropologist Alexander von Gernet, "some aspect of the infant's underdeveloped soul configuration was deemed recyclable and that the Huron attempted to control the fate of this aspect through a strategic placement of the corpse." [138]

Among some Native American groups, such as the Northern Athapaskan Dene Tha, the soul is regarded as a dual entity. The soul is believed to remain in the afterworld and can be prayed to and, at the same time, exists in the human form of the reincarnated individual, also known as "Those Made Again."

---

[136] St. Pierre, Mark and Tilda Long Soldier. *Walking in the Sacred Manner*. New York: Touchstone Books 1995, 99.

[137] Mills, Antonia. "Reincarnation and Survival." A paper given at Survival of Bodily Death, An Esalen Invitational Conference, February 11-16, 2000.

[138] Von Gernet, Alexander. "Saving the Souls: Reincarnation Beliefs of the Seventeenth-Century Huron" in *Amerindian Rebirth: Reincarnation Belief Among North American Indians and Inuit*. Ed. by Anotnia Mills and Richard Slobodin. Toronto: University of Toronto Press 1994, 47.

In many Native American societies, specific lullabies were sung to infants to deal with reincarnation and to ease the "old soul" into the new body. Herbert Spinden noted, "The Eskimo and several other northern tribes believe that the soul of a dead relative enters into a new born child and watches over it during its tender years. This person may be addressed, therefore, in the child's lullaby and, vice versa, the child's prattling tongue may drop words of wisdom, thanks to the experienced soul." [139]

One lullaby sung by the Haida Indians of Queen Charlotte Island, according to Spinden, "apologizes for the mean life of the present as compared with the exalted past; it is addressed to an old woman whose spiritual personality continued its existence in a baby girl." [140]

Over time, the child forgets its past as the soul becomes used to its present situation and life. The memories fade away to nothingness.

In some instances, the reincarnated soul passes from the human existence to animal form. This is not common however, as four times more human to human transmigrations are reported than human to animal forms. Animal incarnations were commonly believed to occur among the Kwakiutl, Zuni and Mohave. The Zuni and Mohave believed that a human spirit was incarnated four times in a series of animal and insect births. At each incarnation, the spirit became more powerful. Such animal-insect transformations were said to be temporary with human incarnations remaining part of the cycle. Some Native American cultures believed that animal transformations were reserved only for bad people. The Yurok, according to 19th century ethnologist Stephen Powers, "fully believe in the transmigration of souls; that they return to earth as birds, squirrels, rabbits, or other feeble animals liable to be harried and devoured. It is more especially the wicked who are subject to this misfortune as a punishment." [141] The Wintūn of Northern California, according to Powers, believed that the souls of the wicked "return into the grizzly bear, for that is the most evil and odious animal they can conceive of. Hence they will not partake of the flesh of a grizzly,

---

[139] Spinden, Herbert Joseph. *Songs of the Tewa*. Brooklyn Museum 1933, 18.
[140] Ibid.
[141] Powers, Stephen. *Tribes of California*. Berkeley: University of California Press 1976, 59.

lest they should absorb some wicked soul." [142] For the most part, however, reincarnation was viewed as a desirable form of soul continuity, be it in animal or human form.

---

[142] Ibid., 240.

9   Myths & Legends of Ghosts & Death

Why People Die Forever (Blackfoot)

One time Old Man said to Old Woman, "People will never die." Oh! " said Old Woman, "that will never do; because, if people live always, there will be too many people in the world."

"Well," said, Old Man, "we do not want to die forever. We shall die for four days and then come to life again."

"Oh, no!" said Old Woman, "it will be better to die forever, so that we shall be sorry for each other."

"Well," said Old Man, "we will decide this way. We will throw a buffalo chip into the water. If it sinks, we will die forever; if it floats, we shall live again."

"Well," said Old Woman, "throw it in."

Now, Old Woman had great power, and she caused the chip to turn into a stone, so it sank. So when we die, we die forever. [143]

---

[143] Wissler, Clark and D. C. Duvall, *Mythology of the Blackfoot Indians* (New York: Anthropological Papers of the American Museum of Natural History, 1908), v. 2, part 1, p. 21.

The Doctrine of Souls (Chinook)

When a person is sick, the seers go and visit the ghosts. Three or four are sent. One who has a powerful guardian spirit goes first; another one who has a powerful guardian spirit goes last; the less powerful ones goes in the middle. They go to search for the soul of the sick chief. Their guardian spirits go to the country of the ghosts. When their road becomes dangerous, the first one sings his song. When danger approaches from the rear, the last one sings his song. They begin their ceremonies in the evening, and when the morning star rises they reach the soul of the sick person. They take it and return. Sometimes it takes them two nights to find the soul. As soon as they return it the patient recovers. [144]

[144] Hardin, Terri, ed. *Legends & Lore of the American Indians.* New York: Barnes & Noble, Inc. 1993, 421.

A Tachi Yokut Myth

Tachi had a fine wife who died and was buried. Her husband went to her grave and dug a hole near it. There he stayed watching, not eating, using only tobacco. After two nights he saw that she came up, brushed the earth off herself, and started to go to the island of the dead. The man tried to seize her but could not hold her. She went southeast and he followed her. Whenever he tried to hold her she escaped. He kept trying to seize her, however, and delayed her. At daybreak she stopped. He stayed there, but could not see her. When it began to be dark the woman got up again and went on. She turned westward and crossed Tulare Lake (or its inlet). At daybreak the man again tried to seize her but could not hold her. She stayed in the place during the day. The man remained in the same place, but again he could not see her. There was a good trail there, and he could see the footprints of his dead friend and relatives. In the evening his wife got up again and went on. They came to a river which flows westward towards San Luis Obispo, the river of the Tulamni (the description fits the Santa Maria, but the Tulamni are in the Tulare drainage, on and about Buena Vista lake). There the man caught up with his wife and there they stayed all day. He still had nothing to eat. In the evening she went on again, now northward. Then somewhere to the west of the Tachi country he caught up with her once more and they spent the day there. In the evening the woman got up and they went on northward, across the San Joaquin river, to the north or east of it. Again he overtook his wife. Then she said: 'What are you going to do? I am nothing now. How can you get my body back? Do you think you shall be able to do it?' He said: 'I think so.' She said: 'I think not. I am going to a different kind of a place now.' From daybreak on that man stayed there. In the evening the woman started once more and went down along the river; but he overtook her again. She did not talk to him. Then they stayed all day, and at night went on again.

Now they were close to the island of the dead. It was joined to the land by a rising and falling bridge called *ch'eleli*. Under this bridge a river ran swiftly. The dead passed over this. When they were on the bridge, a bird suddenly fluttered up beside them and frightened them. Many fell off into the river, where they turned into fish. Now the chief of the dead said: 'Somebody has come.' They told him: 'There are two. One of them is alive; he stinks.' The chief said: 'Do not let him cross.' When the woman came on the island, he asked her: 'You have a companion?' and she told him: 'Yes, my husband.' He asked her: 'Is he coming here?' She said, 'I do not know. He is alive.' They asked the man: 'Do you want to come to this country?' He said: 'Yes,' Then they told him: 'Wait, I will see the chief.' They told the chief: 'He says that he wants to come to this country. We think he does not tell the truth.' 'Well, let him come across.' Now they intended to frighten him off the bridge. They said: 'Come on. The chief says you can cross.' Then the bird *(kacha)* flew up and tried to scare him', but did not make him fall off the bridge into the water. So they brought him before the chief. The chief said: 'This is a bad country. You should *not* have come. We have only your wife's soul *(itit)*. She has left her bones with her body. I do not think we can give her back to you.' In the evening they danced. It was a round dance and they shouted. The chief said to the man: 'Look at your wife in the middle of the crowd. Tomorrow you will see no one.' Now the man stayed there three days. Then the chief said to some of the people: 'Bring that woman. Her husband wants to talk to her.' They brought the woman to him. He asked her: 'Is this your husband?' She said.- 'Yes.' He asked her: 'Do you think you will go back to him?' She said: 'I do not think so. What do you wish?' The chief said: 'I think not. You must stay here. You cannot go back. You are worthless now.' Then he said to the man: 'Do you want to sleep with your wife?' He said: 'Yes, for a while. I want to sleep with her and talk to her.' Then he was allowed to sleep with her that night and they talked together. At daybreak the woman was vanished and he was sleeping next to a fallen oak. The chief said to him: 'Get up. It is late.' He opened his eyes and saw an oak instead of his wife. The chief said: 'You see that we cannot make your wife as she was. She is no good now. It is best that you go back. You have a good country there.' But the man said: 'No, I will stay.' The chief told him: 'No, do not. Come back here whenever you like, but go back now.' Nevertheless he man stayed there six days. Then he said: 'I am going back.' Then in the morning he started to go home. The chief told him: 'When you arrive, hide yourself. Then after six days emerge and make a dance.' Now the man returned. He told his parents: 'Make me a small house. In six days I will come out and dance.' Now he stayed there five days. Then his friends began to know that he had come back. 'Our relative has come back,' they all said. Now the man was in too much of a hurry. After five days he went out. In the evening he began to dance and danced all night, telling what he saw. In the morning when he had stopped dancing, he went to bathe. Then a rattlesnake bit him. He died. So be went back to island. He is there now. It is through him that the people know it is there. Every two days the island becomes fall. Then the chief gathers the people. 'You must swim,' he says. The people stop dancing and bathe. Then the bird frightens them, and some turn to fish, and some to ducks; only a few come out of the water again as people. In this way room is made when the island is too full. The name of the chief there is Kandjidji. [145]

---

[145] Kroeber, A. L. *Indian Myths of South Central California*, University of California Publications, *American Archaeology and Ethnology*, vol. IV, no. 4 (1906-7), PP. 216-18

The Winnebago Indian Road – Land of the Dead

Before the spirit of the departed starts his Journey to the nether world, he is carefully informed of the surprises and dangers of the voyage and is duly instructed how to overcome them. This then, is the story/lessons taught:

I suppose you are not far away, that indeed you are right behind me. Here is the tobacco and here is the pipe which you must keep in front of you as you go along. Here also are the fire and the food which your relatives have prepared for your journey.

In the morning when the sun rises you are to start. You will not have gone very far before you come to a wide road. That is the road you must take. As you go along you will notice something on your road. Take your war club and strike it and throw it behind you. Then go on without looking back. As you go farther you will again come across some obstacle. Strike it and throw it behind you and do not look back. Farther on you will come across some animals, and these also you must strike and throw behind you. Then go on and do not look back. The objects you throw behind you will come to those relatives whom you have left behind you on earth. They will represent victory in war, riches, and animals for food.

When you have gone but a short distance from the last place where you threw the objects behind, you will come to a round lodge and there you will find an old woman. She is the one who is to give you further information. She will ask you, "Grandson, what is your name?"

This you must tell her. Then you must say, "Grandmother, when I was about to start from the earth I was given the following objects with which I was to act as mediator between you and the human beings [i.e., the pipe, tobacco, and food]." Then you must put the stem of the pipe in the old woman's mouth and say, "Grandmother, I have made all my relatives lonesome, my parents, my brothers, and all the others. I would therefore like to have them obtain victory in war, and honours. That was my desire as I left them downhearted upon the earth. I would that they could have all that life which I left behind me on earth. This is what they asked. This, likewise, they asked me, that they should not have to travel on this road for some time to come. They also asked to be blessed with those things that people are accustomed to have on earth. All this they wanted me to ask of you when I started from, the earth. They told me to follow the four steps that would be imprinted with blue marks, Grandmother."

"Well, grandson, you are young but you are wise. It is good. I will now boil some food for you." Thus she will speak to you and then put a kettle on the fire and boil some rice for you. If you eat it you will have a headache. Then she will say, "Grandson, you have a headache, let me cup it for you." Then she will break open your skull and take out your brains and you will forget all about your people on earth and where you came from. You will not worry about your relatives. You will become like a holy spirit. Your thoughts will not go as far as the earth, as there will be nothing carnal about you.

Now the rice that the old woman will boil will really be lice. For that reason you will be finished with everything evil. Then you will go on stepping in the four footsteps mentioned before and that were imprinted with blue earth. You are to take the four steps because the road will fork there. All your relatives who died before you will be there.

As you journey on you will come to a fire running across the earth from one end to the other. There will be a bridge across it but it will be difficult to cross because it is continually swinging. However, you will be able to cross it safely, for you have all the guides about whom the warriors spoke to you. They will take you over and take care of you.

Well, we have told you a good road to take. If anyone tells a falsehood in speaking of the spirit-road, you will fall off the bridge and be burned. However you need not worry for you will pass over safely. As you proceed from that place the spirits will come to meet you and take you to the village where the chief lives. There you will give him the tobacco and ask for those objects of which we spoke to you, the same you asked of the old woman. There you will meet all the relatives that died before you. They will be living in a large lodge. This you must enter. [146]

---

[146] Paul Radin, The Winnebago Tribe, in Thirty-eighth Annual Report, Bureau of American Ethnology (Washington, D.C., 1923), PP. 143-4

The Camp of the Ghosts (Blackfoot)

There was once a man who loved his wife dearly. After they had been married for a time they had a little boy. Some time after that the woman grew sick and did not get well. She was sick for a long time. The young man loved his wife so much that he did not wish to take a second woman. The woman grew worse and worse. Doctoring did not seem to do her any good. At last she died.

For a few days after this, the man used to take his baby on his back and travel out away from the camp, walking over the hills, crying and mourning. He felt badly, and he did not know what to do.
After a time he said to the little child, "My little boy, you will have to go and live with your grandmother. I shall go away and try to find your mother and bring her back."

He took the baby to his mother's lodge and asked her to take care of it and left it with her. Then he started away, not knowing where he was going nor what he should do.

When he left the camp, he travelled toward the Sand Hills. On the fourth night of his journeying he had a dream. He dreamed that he went into a little lodge in which was an old woman. This old woman said to him, "Why are you here, my son?"

The young man replied, "I am mourning day and night, crying all the while. My little son, who is the only one left me, also mourns."

"Well," asked the old woman, "for whom are you mourning?"

The young man answered, "I am mourning for my wife. She died some time ago. I am looking for her."

"Oh, I saw her," said the old woman; "she passed this way. I myself have no great power to help you, but over by that far butte beyond, lives another old woman. Go to her and she will give you power to continue your journey. You could not reach the place you are seeking without help. Beyond the next butte from her lodge you will find the camp of the ghosts."

The next morning the young man awoke and went on toward the next butte. It took him a long summer's day to get there, but he found there no lodge, so he lay down and slept. Again he dreamed. In his dream he saw a little lodge, and saw an old woman come to the door and heard her call to him. He went into the lodge, and she spoke to him.

"My son, you are very unhappy. I know why you have come this way. You are looking for your wife who is now in the ghost country. It is a very hard thing for you to get there. You may not be able to get your wife back, but I have great power and I will do for you all that I can. If you act as I advise, you may succeed."

Other wise words she spoke to him, telling him what he should do; also she gave him a bundle of mysterious things which would help him on his journey.

She went on to say, "You stay here for a time and I will go over there to the ghosts' camp and try to bring back some of your relations who are there. If it is possible for me to bring them back, you may return there with them, but on the way you must shut your eyes. If you should open them and look about you, you would die. Then you would never come back. When you come to the camp you will pass by a big lodge and they will ask you, 'Where are you going and who told you to come here?' You must answer, 'My grandmother, who is standing out here with me, told me to come.' They will try to scare you; they will make fearful noises and you will see strange and terrible things, but do not be afraid."

The old woman went away, and after a time came back with one of the man's relations. He went with this relation to the ghosts' camp. When they came to the large lodge some one called out and asked the man what he was doing there, and he answered as the old woman had told him. As he passed on through the camp the ghosts tried to frighten him with many fearful sights and sounds, but he kept up a strong heart.

Presently he came to another lodge, and the man who owned it came out and spoke to him, asking where he was going. The young man said, "I am looking for my dead wife. I mourn for her so much that I cannot rest. My little boy too keeps crying for his mother. They have offered to give me other wives, but I do not want them. I want the one for whom I am searching."

The ghost said, "It is a fearful thing that you have come here; it is very likely that you will never go away. Never before has there been a person here."

The ghost asked him to come into his lodge, and he entered.
This chief ghost said to him, "You shall stay here for four nights and you shall see your wife, but you must be very careful or you will never go back. You will die here in this very place."

Then the chief ghost walked out of the lodge and shouted out for a feast, inviting the man's father-in-law and other relations who were in the camp to come and eat, saying, "Your son-in-law invites you to a feast," as if he meant that the son-in-law had died and become a ghost and arrived at the camp of the ghosts.

Now when these invited ghosts had reached the lodge they did not like to go in. They said to each other, "There is a person here"; it seemed as if they did not like the smell of a human being. The chief ghost burned sweet pine on the fire, which took away this smell, and then the ghosts came in and sat down.

The chief ghost said to them, "Now pity this son-in-law of yours. He is looking for his wife. Neither the great distance that he has come nor the fearful sights that he has seen here have weakened his heart. You can see how tender-hearted he is. He not only mourns because he has lost his wife, but he mourns because his little boy is now alone, with no mother; so pity him and give him back his wife."

The ghosts talked among themselves, and one of them said to the man, "Yes; you shall stay here for four nights, and then we will give you a medicine pipe—the Worm Pipe—and we will give you back your wife and you may return to your home."

Now, after the third night the chief ghost called together all the people, and they came, and with them came the man's wife. One of the ghosts was beating a drum, and following him was another who carried the Worm Pipe, which they gave to him.

Then the chief ghost said, "Now be very careful; to-morrow you and your wife will start on your journey homeward. Your wife will carry the medicine pipe and for four days some of your relations will go along with you. During this time you must keep your eyes shut; do not open them, or you will return here and be a ghost forever. Your wife is not now a person. But in the middle of the fourth day you will be told to look, and when you have opened your eyes you will see that your wife has become a person, and that your ghost relations have disappeared."

Before the man went away his father-in-law spoke to him and said, "When you get near home you must not go at once into the camp. Let some of your relations know that you have come, and ask them to build a sweat-house for you. Go into that sweat-house and wash your body thoroughly, leaving no part of it, however small, uncleansed. If you fail in this, you will die. There is something about the ghosts that it is difficult to remove. It can only be removed by a thorough sweat. Take care now that you do what I tell you. Do not whip your wife, nor strike her with a knife, nor hit her with fire. If you do, she will vanish before your eyes and return here."

They left the ghost country to go home, and on the fourth day the wife said to her husband, "Open your eyes." He looked about him and saw that those who had been with them had disappeared, and he found that they were standing in front of the old woman's lodge by the butte. She came out of her lodge and said to them, "Stop; give me back those mysterious medicines of mine, whose power helped you to do what you wished." The man returned them to her, and then once more became really a living person.

When they drew near to the camp the woman went on ahead and sat down on a butte. Then some curious persons came out to see who this might be. As they approached the woman called out to them, "Do not come any nearer. Go and tell my mother and my relations to put up a lodge for us a little way from the camp, and near by it build a sweat-house." When this had been done the man and his wife went in and took a thorough sweat, and then they went into the lodge and burned sweet grass and purified their clothing and the Worm Pipe. Then their relations and friends came in to see them. The man told them where he had been and how he had managed to get his wife back, and that the pipe hanging over the doorway was a medicine pipe—the Worm Pipe—presented to him by his ghost father-in-law.

That is how the people came to possess the Worm Pipe. That pipe belongs to the band of Piegans known as the Worm People.

Not long after this, once in the night, this man told his wife to do something, and when she did not begin at once he picked up a brand from the fire and raised it—not that he intended to strike her with it, but he made as if he would—when all at once she vanished and was never seen again. [147]

---

[147] Grinnell, George Bird .Blackfeet Indian Stories. New York: Charles Scribner's Sons 1913

Why People Die (Paiute)

In the Owens Valley Paiute myth, "Why People Die" Coyote and Wolf argue about whether or not the elderly should be able to climb Bald Mountain to bathe in the sacred spring found at the top. By bathing in these waters, the elderly become young again and never die. Coyote believed that people should die when they reach old age but Wolf thought otherwise. Coyote became so angry "that he kicked Bald Mountain and it toppled over into the valley below." The magical waters were destroyed and death was created.[148]

---

[148] Riddell, Francis A. *Honey Lake Paiute Ethnography.* Carson City: Nevada State Museum Anthropological Papers #4 1960, 80

Appendix:
The Shadow or Ghost Lodge [149]

The ceremonies here described were witnessed among the Ogallala Indians in 1882. The old men of the tribe told me that formerly a period of two years was necessary to fulfill the requirements of this rite. Now six months or a year will suffice.

These Indians entertain the belief that after death the soul will linger near the body so long as it is preserved or any part of it kept intact, particularly if not exposed to the air. The clothing too, which was needful to the comfort of the body, partakes of the individuality of the person and the spirit will linger about these articles. On account of this belief the personal belongings are always placed with the body of the dead, and an Indian will never consciously wear any article of clothing which has been used by one who is deceased. This idea that the soul lingers near any part of the body which is carefully preserved is closely connected with the Shadow or Ghost Lodge. The name was explained as referring to the soul being like a shadow continually with the body and at death gradually fading away.

A ghost lodge is usually kept for a child. The rites are initiated by the father who is the principal actor and responsible person in all the ceremonies. It is creditable to have kept a lodge of this character, and the public consideration seems to arise the general respect paid to any especial honoring of the dead as giving proof of family faithfulness and affection, as well as the accumulation of wealth by the father, and the characteristic disposition of it. It is by such deeds that a man gains tribal distinction, and favors his advance to public office. These preferments won from the tribe by an Indian proving his devotion to the religious ceremonies and

---

[149] Fletcher, Alice. The Shadow or Ghost Lodge: A Ceremony of the Oglala Sioux. *Peabody Museum Papers* 3: 296-307, 1882.

traditions of his fathers, by a faithful fulfillment of certain rites, as well as by showing prowess in action and wisdom in counsel.

If, on the death of a child, the father desires to keep a ghost lodge, he speedily sends for a holy or "wakan-man," who on his arrival at the father's tent, takes a pipe, which is handed him, and fills it chanting a ritual suitable to the occasion. One of the criers of the camp is called and he receives the pipe and starts for the tent of a man who has successfully kept a ghost lodge. As the crier enters the tent he says in an intoning voice : (FN1)

"The one who sends me wishes to keep a ghost lodge," and offers the pipe. The man addressed accepts the pipe, lights it, and smokes it in silence. When it is finished he goes to the father's tent where the child lies dead.

After entering the tent and observing a brief silence the man sent for walks over to where the child lies dressed in its best clothing, its face painted red, and taking a knife cuts off a lock of hair just above the forehead. He then hands the hair to the mother, who takes it, wraps it in a piece of new cloth, and lays it away, where it remains undisturbed for four days. Skin was formerly used in place of cloth.

Four yards of red cloth are divided into two parts. One part is carried out beyond the camp, to an elevation if possible, and buried in a hole about three feet deep. This is an offering to the earth, and the chanted prayer asks that the life, or flower in the earth, will help the father in keeping successfully all the requirements of the ghost lodge. The other part of the red cloth is lifted and offered to the buffalo, with a prayer that good may be granted to the father during the period of the lodge-keeping. After this ceremony the cloth is cut into eight strips and given to eight men who have successfully kept a ghost lodge. This is a request for their good will and help. Formerly a deerskin, well tanned and painted red, was thus offered. These ceremonies are performed by the wakan-man and the man who cut the child's hair.

The dancing society to which the father belongs present him with horses, and friends make gifts; these are all treasured against the day of final ceremonies. After these preliminaries the body of the child is put away with the usual burial rites.

The duties of the father begin at the time the hair is cut and continue until the closing ceremonies, six months or a year afterwards. During this interval he cannot eat dog meat or any flesh scraped from the skin or hide of an animal. He cannot cut open the head of any animal to get the brains, strike or break any ribs or do any butchering. He cannot take a gun, pistol, arrows, or any weapon in his hand. He cannot run, go in swimming, make any violent movement, shake a blanket, his clothing, or in any way disturb the air. No one must pass before him or touch him, and to prevent this disaster a coal of fire is always kept about two feet in front of him as he sits in the tent. Although he remains with his family he must live apart from his wife, and on no account take a child in his arms, for if he should so forget himself the child would surely die. (FN2)

During the four days the hair is laid away the mother and sisters, or the near female relatives, make a small buckskin bag in which the hair is to be placed. A pack of the same material or cloth is prepared, having buckskin thongs with which to tie it. A new tent is pitched not far from the father's tent, the opening toward the east. Formerly this tent for the ghost lodge was set a little within the tribal circle or open space, out from the line of living tents.

On the fourth day the wakan-man, and the man who had cut the hair from the child, repair to the tent set apart for the lodge, and make up the pack into a roll about six inches in diameter and two feet long, enclosing the buckskin bag containing the lock of hair cut from the child, and the pipe which had been filled by the wakan-man and sent out by the father. To these are added any other articles which the parents may choose to contribute. Three crotched sticks had been cut by a male relative, and for the honor of doing this he had given away the value of a horse. On these sticks the pack is tied. A fire (fig. 1, a) is made in the centre of the tent, back of which an oval is drawn upon the ground about three feet in diameter, having an elongated opening at the east (fig. 1, b). The sod is then removed from within the figure and the earth thus exposed is mellowed and made fine. Down from the wild goose, colored with red ochre, is placed along the outline of the figure. [FN 3] Behind the oval figure the three crotched sticks are set up having the pack fastened to them where they come together (fig. 1, c). A bowl and a wooden spoon are fastened to the outside of the pack.

[Figure.1]

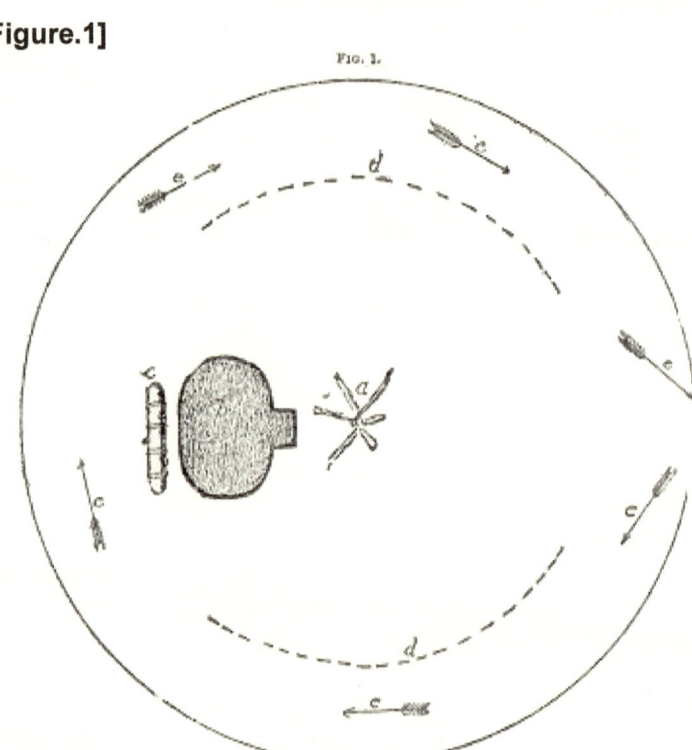

Fig. 1.

Arrangement of the ghost lodge at the beginning of the ceremony.

No woman but the mother of the child is allowed to enter this tent. She has charge of the pack, but can only pass into the tent when performing some duty incident to the lodge-keeping. When entering the tent she turns to the left and makes the entire circle, always going behind the pack and passing out by the right. This mode of entering and leaving is observed by all who enter the tent, and is indicated by the arrows in the diagram (fig. 1, e.) No one may pass between the pack and the symbol drawn on the ground, or between that and the fire. [FN 4] Nor can any one turn back on his passage round the tent, for one must always move in a continuous circle from left to right. On clear sunny days, when the wind does not blow, the mother carries the crotched sticks, with the pack tied to them, outside the tent, setting them up about four or five feet in front of the entrance. As the sun declines she returns the pack to its place in the tent. When it thunders, or if a gun should be fired, or any unwonted noise should be heard, she must hasten to cover the pack. If, when the pack is out of doors, a sudden wind should rise, the mother must instantly take the pack into the tent. Thus her constant care is necessary.

Every day the father of the child enters the ghost lodge tent and the mother, soon after, sets kettles of food inside the tent door. The father loosens the dish from the pack, a small quantity of the food is placed in it, and the dish set down near the pack. The father then takes a bit of the food from the dish with his fingers and, lifting it, says : " We offer this food that you may help us, that we may escape ill fortune. We ask you to help us to avoid any sickness or misfortune that may lie in our path." [FN 5] The offering is then dropped upon the mellowed earth and buried in it. During this ceremony persons of the male sex may be present; their position on the north and south side of the lodge is indicated on the diagram by the letter d. It is usual for orphans, the aged, or any one in need of food, to repair to the ghost lodge to share in this daily feast given by the father as a religious hospitality.

In the tent certain rules must be observed ; the mode of entering, moving about and leaving have been already mentioned. No one may blow the fire with his mouth. When it needs to be livened one may gently fan it with the wing of a bird, but in no other way: no one may spit toward the centre of the tent, but if he needs to cast anything from his mouth, he must turn his head and throw the saliva behind him. No tales of fighting, nor any quarrelsome words, nor any subject which is "bad" must be spoken in a ghost lodge. Quietness and friendliness must pervade the tent.

If at any time during the period of keeping the lodge the father should by accident hear of any violent words or deeds, he must at once perform certain rites which will avert the evil consequences to him and his family. He must take a few coals of fire, and lay on them a bunch of sweet grass, or sprays of cedar. As the smoke rises he must crouch over the coals bringing his blanket close about his body, drawing it over his head and face so as completely to shut him in with the smoke; sitting thus while the aromatic fumes circle his entire person, he thinks of the duty of carefully fulfilling the ritual of the religious ceremony and by his faithfulness arresting disaster and securing good fortune for his kin.

During the months occupied with these duties the man can do little more than fulfill them. As he is barred from bunting and providing food and raiment, his needs are supplied by his kindred. It is not enough that his avocations should be peaceful but it is his duty to relinquish any hard feeling he has had and forget old injuries. The keeping of a ghost lodge is a signal of peace and cancels all grudges between parties. The father may not smoke with any one lest he should consort with a man who was at emnity with some other person. The Indians in explanation pointed out that it was for the purpose of enforcing peace in a man's actions and thoughts that he was forbidden to take weapons in his hand ; and the coal of fire placed before him while sitting in his tent was indicative of his setting himself apart for this religious duty, "the coal being like a partition between the father and all the world."

During these intermediate months, the family are busily employed making eagle war bonnets, embroidering moccasins, tobacco pouches, tobacco boards, fashioning pipes and ornamenting clothing and gathering together a large amount of possessions to be given away at the closing ceremonies. After a ghost lodge a family are often left in poverty, but with the Indians it is not accumulation and hoarding, but the record of that which a man has given away which entitles him to greatness and influence.

Any one of the same gens[FN 6] as the father, who had lost a child, after the ghost lodge had been inaugurated and who desired to join in the ceremony, could prepare a similar pack, and tie it to the one in the ghost lodge. Each family thus represented must contribute its quota of gifts at the final day.

As that time draws near word is sent abroad, inviting members of other gens, and even of other tribes, to be present and participate in the feast. Four days the crier proclaims the opening of the packs and distribution of the gifts, and during these days the families are busy preparing for the coming feast. A man who has successfully kept a ghost lodge is invited to take charge of the proceedings. For this service he receives large presents from the parents represented in the lodge. To give an idea of this payment the following list of articles was received by the man having charge of the ghost lodge herein described.

Four garnished buffalo robes embroidered with porcupine quills, four woven sashes, four calico shirts, four pipes, four plugs of tobacco, four hatchets, six pairs of moccasins, six dishes, six tin pans, seven yards of calico (a dress pattern), ten butcher knives, two pairs of leggings, two strings of bells, two curtains (strips of tent cloth used to protect the sleeping place), two comforters (bed quilts), one lariat, one hoe, one bed made of reeds, one steer, two or three ponies.

Among the articles given away, the following were counted.

Thirty-two ponies, one hundred pairs of moccasins, ten shawls, seven buffalo robes, three war bonnets (eagle feathers), eight calico dresses (made up), besides numerous tin pails and cups, knives, coffee pots, tin pans, looking glasses such as the young men wear, embroidered beaded dresses, knife cases, match pockets, bows and arrows, wooden bowls, balls, shinny sticks embroidered with beads, a quantity of dried cherries, squash, pounded meat and other things.

From early morning to well on toward noon the women were engaged carrying these gifts singly, in packs made of raw hide, or in wooden trunks, and placing them at the door of the new tent set up to receive them. On this final day all signs of mourning are put away, for the first time since the death occurred the immediate relatives braid their hair, and every one is in gala dress. Over 800 people gathered to the feast, and were scattered over the grass. Forty-two great kettles hung from crotched sticks, the beef soup and dog stew flavored with dried cherries or turnips sent up fumes of steam. The sticks used to stir these viands were forked, having the end ornamented with beads and ribbons. Young girls were bringing water from the creek, the older ones grinding coffee, and all busy preparing for the great crowd of guests. The abrupt outline of the buttes, dark evergreens marking the gullies, the narrow valley through which flowed the clear rapid creek with its border of shrubs and large graceful trees, the green bottom lands dotted with white tents, while a few were scattered over the hills that rose in terraces to the east, together with the vast throngs of gayly dressed Indians, combined to make a picture full of color, spirit, and a wild beauty all its own, bearing no familiar lines to eastern civilized eyes.

[Figure.2]

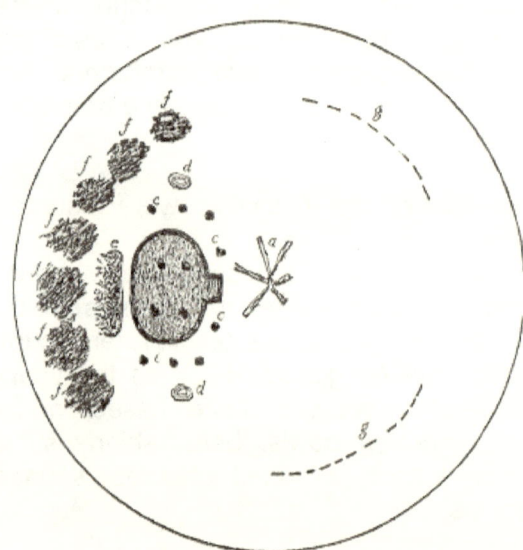

Arrangement of the tent set up to receive the gifts.

The new tent set up for the reception of the gifts (fig. 2) is placed near the ghost lodge tent, the door facing the east. Near the centre a fire is kindled (fig. 2, a), an oval figure drawn on the ground (fig. 2, b) similar to that cut on the floor of the ghost lodge. The sod is removed from within the figure, the earth mellowed, four live coals laid on the mellowed earth and sweet grass dropped on them. Outside the figure eight coals are placed, four on each side (fig. 2, c), and sweet grass laid on to smoulder. [FN 7] On the north and south side a buffalo chip is set (fig. 2, d). Back of the oval figure the sod is removed so as to leave a narrow, oblong figure in the earth on which Sprays of Artemisia are spread like a mat (fig. 2, e) ; behind this the presents are arranged in piles (fig. 2,f), one pile for each ghost represented in the lodge. [FN 8]

After this arrangement is completed a feast is given and while that is in progress the women set a row of crotched sticks in front of the tent, laying on poles to form a framework, on which they spread for exhibition the gifts they had previously made into piles at the back of the tent. When the feast is concluded, the master of ceremonies distributes these gifts, reserving those which are to be given away in the ghost lodge tent. Visitors and the poor are remembered in the lavish bestowal.

[Figure.3]

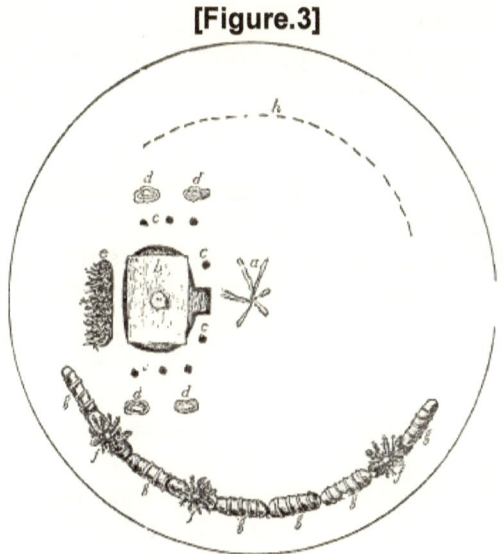

Arrangement of the ghost lodge at the concluding stage of the ceremony.

The interior of the ghost lodge (fig. 3) is rearranged in the following manner. The space occupied by the packs is marked off in an oblong, the sod removed and the ground spread with Artemisia (fig. 3, e). The figure having the mellowed earth in which the offerings of food have been buried each day, is covered with a red cloth. On the centre is laid a disk of shell (fig. 3, b) ; eight live coals, four on each side, are arranged outside the figure, and sweet grass laid on them (fig. 3, c). Four buffalo chips are outside of these at the four corners (fig. 3, d). The different packs are loosened from the initial pack and each one fastened to sticksabout four feet long. There were nine packs, three belonging to young men (fig. 3, f), three to boys, two to girls and one to a woman (fig. 3, g). The sticks are bound with hide, and an oblong piece of hide, ornamented and having on it, a face rudely outlined in paint, is hung in front of each pack. Upon the packs belonging to the young men are fastened eagle feather war bonnets. These effigies are arranged in a semicircle on the south side of the tent, the sticks being thrust in the ground, and the gifts contributed by the relations of the dead person piled about his effigy.

Only men who have kept a ghost lodge are entitled to sit in this tent, and join in smoking the pipe which had been filled with the appropriate ritual. Their position is indicated in fig. 3 by the letter h. The man in charge of the ceremonies distributes the gifts which rest about the effigies to the men present. In so doing he is particular so to dispose of the articles as, for instance, to avoid giving an eagle war bonnet to a man who had received one on a previous and similar occasion. Such items are well remembered in an Indian camp, for it is in this way that possessions change hands. The men who receive at this time will save up their treasures and give them away at some future religious or secular festival.

When all the gifts are distributed the packs are opened, the pipes are given to poor men, and the hair once more handed back to the mother who either keeps it, or buries it, and the soul of the child, which bas been supposed to linger about the pack, is now free to depart.

The shadows were gathering in the valley and the last glow fading from the buttes, as the tents fell and the poles were gathered and carried off by their possessors, for not an article used in this strange ceremonial remained in the possession of the parents who had thus paid to the full their tribute of affection for the dead, and proved themselves faithful to the custom of their ancestors. The stars came out and shone over the silent plains, for the men, women and children had vanished with the day.

Footnotes

Footnote 1 -The prayers and rituals are chanted or intoned. When the latter is used the breath is audibly inhaled, something as it to during ceremonial smoking. All ceremonial addresses and announcements by the criers are given in a key differing from the natural tone of voice. This is the conventional manner, and is often unconsciously adopted on ordinary occasions.

Footnote 2 -An Indian who was keeping a ghost lodge attended the sun dance. One day while there he forgot the duties of the ghost lodge and suffered his six year old daughter to approach him, and took her in his arms. Too late he recalled the penalty he had incurred. A fortnight later when I entered his tent, where he was sitting with the coal of fire before him, I saw the little girl lying sick unto death, on the opposite side of the fire. Bending over the child it was evident that she was beyond any medical aid. Her father accepted her fate as a punishment he had merited. Her mother was equally hopeless and sat without, working on moccasins to be given away on the approaching dual Ceremonies, while her brothers and sisters were racing over the hills pictures of careless health. It was a striking scene. To every inquiry I made as to the cause of the child's illness, cold, fever, or the like, the invariable answer given by relative or acquaintance was: "Her father forgot and took her in his arms." It was impossible to present to the people any natural cause for the child's illness, from that which was so clearly another evidence, supernaturally given of the sanctity and power of their religious ceremonies. Next day the child died, leaving her parents full sore at heart.

Footnote 3 -Here again is met the U-ma-ne, which occurs in every festival so far met with, as also the down of the wild goose, and ochre. The constant recurrence of certain symbols and articles used in religious ceremonies indicates lines for the careful investigation of students.

Footnote 4 -The spaced here mentioned are always considered as consecrated or set apart in every ceremony I have witnessed or learned about, and this applies to many tribes.

Footnote 5 -This is the usual form of asking a blessing. This ceremony takes place at every feast, dance or ritual observance whore food is eaten. The father does not address the ghost pack, but the deity or life of the animal food.

Footnote 6 -It was only the Indians of one gens or clan who joined in this ghost lodge. Further Investigation will prove whether this is always the rule among tribes which hold similar lodges.

Footnote 7 -The protective purification and consecration, secured by fire and sweet or aromatic smoke is noticeable throughout this ceremonial, and the number of small fires and their positions seem to indicate a connection with the worship of the four quarters or winds.

Footnote 8 -The traditions concerning the ghost lodge are as follows: Long ago the Dakotas lived in one village and had seven council fires. When they broke up and parted each division received certain gifts. To these particular Indians were given the pipe and the mystery of the ghost lodge. One version says: Two warriors were returning to the camp, when they were met by a woman who said: "When you return, cause a tent to be pitched within the line of tents, and I will come and tell you what to do in the tent." Although alarmed at being thus accosted, the warriros did as they were directed, and the woman came as she had promised. They entered the tent with her and she then revealed the mystery of the ghost lodge, and gave then a pipe, saying: "When you cease to do in this way I have told you, the people will no longer live." She left the tent and vanished in a cloud. Still another version states, that one day there was a woman, wearing an apron of Artemisia, and wrapped in a buffalo skin having the hair outside and the horns left on. She was holding the head in her left hand and the tail in her right, her left hand crossed over the right, and on her left arm she had a buffalo calf, together with a pipe, the two lying side by side. Four days site tarried with the Dakotas and taught them how to keep the ghost lodge, and left them with the words: "when a mule shall bear a foal then will come the destruction of the earth." Some Indians declare that if the father faithfully performs all the duties and ceremonies of the ghost lodge he thereby averts from his child any punishment or bad consequences which would result from misfortunes or disasters received in this life.

In these accounts it is both curious and instructive to note the traces of the early missionaries interwoven with native tradition.

Conclusion

How people treat their dead is very indicative of how they view life. The Roman poet Lucan stated, "Death is the middle of a long life." The Native American held similar views. While ghosts were feared due to the very real possibility of them causing harm to the living, the spirit, the soul was deeply revered. Extreme measures were undertaken to ensure that the spirit of the deceased traveled on to the afterlife without fear of deprivation knowing that their survivors grieved for them and loved them. Grave goods included those daily necessities of life, including utensils, food and possessions that were prized in life. Elaborate, lengthy and expensive ceremonies were observed to assure the soul that it was ok for them to go on.

Many believe that the soul returns in another incarnation, sometimes in the same family, sometimes in another form. All of the beliefs discussed in this small book and many of the ritual-ceremonial practices continue to be observed today—and not only by Native Americans. Native American beliefs concerning the afterworld are similar to other beliefs around the world, including the Celtic Otherworld and the Judeo-Christian heaven, they illustrate the commonality of belief among most cultures. To the Native American there is a world much like our own after death and we do continue on in much the same manner as we do in life. I believe we take comfort in that and in the possibility of being with our loved ones once again.

All of us have the same fears, uncertainties and expectations in life as well as in death. The survival of the soul was a given in Native American traditions. Anthropologist Marie Mauzé stated, "The soul is what animates a body, and it not only stands to body as energy to substance but it also brings humanness to it." [150]

I do not believe that any of us can dispute this statement.

---

[150] Mauzé, Marie. "The Concept of the Person and Reincarnation among the Kwakiutl Indians" in *Amerindian Rebirth: Reincarnation Belief Among North American Indians and Inuit.* Toronto: University of Toronto Press 1990, 180.

About the Author

Gary R. Varner has over twenty books in print about folklore, mythology, Native Americans, ancient symbols, mythic creatures and cultural diffusion. His website, www.authorsden.com/garyrvarner, is visited by readers in over 40 countries. Over 900 university and municipal libraries around the world have copies of his books, including the Smithsonian Institution's Museum of the American Indian and the British Museum.

In an attempt to stay current in folklore studies, he maintains membership in the American Folklore Society and the Royal Anthropological Institute. His articles have appeared in American, British and German journals.

Varner has traveled extensively to document his material, most notably to England, Wales, Ireland, Canada, Yucatan, and across the United States.

Bibliography

Anderson, John. *Kuta Teachings: Reincarnation Theology of the Chumash Indians of California.* Kootenai: American Designs Publishing 1998

Ashton, John and Tom Whyte. *The Quest for Paradise.* New York: HarperSanFrancisco 2001

Balikci, Asen. *The Netsilik Eskimo.* Garden City: The Natural History Press 1970

Bancroft, Hubert H. Nat. Races of Pac. States, 1874 vol. i

Bierhorst, John. *The Mythology of Mexico and Central America.* New York: William Morrow and Company, Inc. 1990

Blackburn, Thomas C. *December's Child: A Book of Chumash Oral Narratives.* Berkeley: University of California Press 1975

Bonwick, James. *Irish Druids and Old Irish Religions.* New York: Barnes & Noble Books 1986. A reprint of the 1894 edition.

Bright, William. "Karok" in *Handbook of North American Indians: Vol. 8-California.* Washington: Smithsonian Institution 1978

Brown, Joseph Epes, ed. *The Sacred Pipe: Black Elk's Account of the Seven Rites of the Oglala Sioux.* Norman: University of Oklahoma Press 1953, 1989

Byrd, William. *History of the Dividing Line*, Vol. 1, 1792 (reprinted 1866)

Campisi, Jack. "The Hudson Valley Indians Through Dutch Eyes" in *Neighbors and Intruders: An Ethnohistorical Exploration of the*

Indians of Hudson's River. Ottawa: Canadian Ethnology Service Paper No. 39, National Museum of Man Mercury Series 1976

Cooper, John M. *Analytical and Critical Bibliography of the Tribes of Tierra del Fuego and Adjacent Territory.* Washington: Smithsonian Institution Bureau of American Ethnology Bulletin 63, 1917

Frazer, Sir James. *The Golden Bough: A study in magic and religion.* Hertfordshire: Wordsworth Editions 1993

Heidenreich, Conrad E. "Huron" in *Handbook of North American Indians, Vol. 15: Northeast.* Washington: Smithsonian Institution 1978

Heizer, Robert F. and Adan E. Treganza. *Mines and Quarries of the Indians of California.* Ramona: Ballena Press 1972

Hoebel, E. Adamson. *The Cheyennes: Indians of the Great Plains.* New York: Holt, Rinehart and Winston, Case Studies in Cultural Anthropology 1960.

Hopkins, Sarah Winnemucca. *Life Among the Piutes.* Reno: University of Nevada Press 1994

Johnston, Bernice Eastman. *California's Gabrielino Indians.* Los Angeles: Southwest Museum 1962

Jones, David E. *Sanapia Comanche Medicine Woman.* New York: Holt, Rinehart and Winston 1972

Kluckhohn, Clyde and Dorothea Leighton. *The Navaho.* Garden City: Anchor Books/The American Museum of Natural History 1962

Krickeberg, Walter et al., *Pre-Columbian American Religions.* New York: Holt, Rinehart and Winston 1968

Krober, A. L. "Elements of Culture in Native California" in *The California Indians*, ed. by R. F. Heizer and M.A. Whipple. Berkeley: University of California Press 1971

Lincoln, Jackson Steward. *The Dream in Native American and Other Primitive Cultures.* Mineola: Dover Publications, Inc. 2003

Lockett, Hattie Greene. "The Unwritten Literature of the Hopi," *Social Science Bulletin Number 2, Vol. IV, Number 4,* May 15, 1933. Tucson: University of Arizona

MacCulloch, J. A. *The Religion of the Ancient Celts.* Mineola: Dover Publications, Inc. 2003

Matthews, Washington. *Ethnological and Philol. Of Hidatsa Indians.* Washington: U.S. Geological and Geographical Survey, Misc. Publications #7, 1877

Mauzé, Marie. "The Concept of the Person and Reincarnation among the Kwakiutl Indians" in *Amerindian Rebirth: Reincarnation Belief Among North American Indians and Inuit.* Toronto: University of Toronto Press 1990, pgs 177-191

Mills, Antonia. "Reincarnation Belief among North American Indians and Inuit: Context, Distribution, and Variation" in *Amerindian Rebirth: Reincarnation Belief Among North American Indians and Inuit.* Toronto: University of Toronto Press 1994, pgs 15-37

Mills, Antonia. "Reincarnation and Survival." A paper given at Survival of Bodily Death, An Esalen Invitational Conference, February 11-16, 2000.

Mooney, James. "The Sacred Formulas of the Cherokees," in *Bureau of American Ethnology, 7th Annual Report, 1885-86.* Washington

Moriarty, James Robert. *Chinigchinix: An Indigenous California Indian Religion.* Los Angeles: Southwest Museum 1969

Ogden, Daniel. *Magic, Witchcraft, and Ghosts in the Greek and Roman Worlds.* Oxford: Oxford University Press 2002

Olmsted, D.L. and Omer C. Stewart. "Achumawi" in *Handbook of North American Indians, Vol. 8: California.* Washington: Smithsonian Institute 1978

Opler, Morris Edward. *An Apache Life-Way: The Economic, Social, and Religious Institutions of the Chiricahua Indians.* Chicago: The University of Chicago Press 1941

Powers, Stephen. *Tribes of California.* Berkeley: University of California Press 1976

Priestly, H. I. *A Historical, Political and Natural Description of California, by Pedro Fages.* Berkeley: University of California Press 1937

Reichard, Gladys A. *Navaho Religion: A Study of Symbolism.* Princeton: Princeton University Press 1950

St. Pierre, Mark and Tilda Long Soldier. *Walking in the Sacred Manner.* New York: Touchstone Books 1995.

Sauter, John and Bruce Johnson. *Tillamook Indians of the Oregon Coast.* Portland: Binfords & Mort, Publishers 1974

Schoolcraft, Henry Rowe. *History of the Indian Tribes of the United States.* Philadelphia: J.B. Lippincott & Co. 1857

Schulz, Paul E. *Indians of Lassen.* Mineral: Loomis Museum Association 1954

Service, Elman R. *Profiles in Ethnography.* New York: Harper & Row, Publishers 1963

Spier, Leslie. *Yuman Tribes of the Gila River.* New York: Dover Publications, Inc. 1978

Spinden, Herbert Joseph. *Songs of the Tewa.* Brooklyn Museum 1933

Stanislawski, Michael B. "Hopi-Tewa" in *Handbook of North American Indians, Vol. 9: Southwest.* Washington: Smithsonian Institute 1978

Steward, Julian H. "Basin-Plateau Aboriginal Sociopolitical Groups" in *Bureau of American Ethnology Bulletin 120.* Washington: Smithsonian Institution 1938

Thomsen, Marie-Louise. "Witchcraft and Magic in Ancient Mesopotamia" in *Witchcraft and Magic in Europe: Biblical and Pagan Societies.* Philadelphia: University of Pennsylvania Press 2001

Varner, Gary R. *The Owens Valley Paiute: A Cultural History.* Morrisville: Lulu Press/OakChylde Books 2009

Von Gernet, Alexander. "Saving the Souls: Reincarnation Beliefs of the Seventeenth-Century Huron" in *Amerindian Rebirth: Reincarnation Belief Among North American Indians and Inuit.* Ed. by Anotnia Mills and Richard Slobodin. Toronto: University of Toronto Press 1994, pgs 38-54

Walker, James R. *Lakota: Belief and Ritual.* Lincoln: University of Nebraska Press 1991

Whiting, Beatrice Blyth. *Paiute Sorcery.* New York: Viking Fund Publications in Anthropology, Number 15, 1950

Whitley, David S. *A Guide to Rock Art Sites: Southern California and Southern Nevada.* Missoula: Mountain Press Publishing Company 1996

Yarrow, H.C. "A further contribution to the study of the mortuary customs of the North American Indians," *First Annual Report of the Bureau of Ethnology to the Secretary of the Smithsonian Institution,* Government Printing Office, Washington, 1881, pages 87-204.

Zigmond, Maurice. "The Supernatural World of the Kawaiisu" in *Flowers of the Wind: Papers on Ritual and Symbolism in California and the Southwest.* Ed. by Thomas C. Blackburn. Socorro: Ballena Press, pp. 59-95.

Illustration Credits

Cover, title page photo and photos on page 4, 15, 70 & 71 by Gary R. Varner

Photo page 27 by Edward S. Curtis, taken between 1907 and 1922

Illustration on page 32, from "United States and Mexican Boundary Survey. Report of William H. Emory..." Washington. 1857

Illustrations on page 42, 43, 44, 46, 47, 48, 49, 50 and 57 are from H.C. Yarrow, "A further contribution to the study of the mortuary customs of the North American Indians," *First Annual Report of the Bureau of Ethnology to the Secretary of the Smithsonian Institution*, Government Printing Office, Washington, 1881, pages 87-204.

Index

www.ingramcontent.com/pod-product-compliance
Lightning Source LLC
Chambersburg PA
CBHW020307290526
45784CB00003B/1393